10
AF183347

DRUG TRANSIT AND DISTRIBUTION, INTERCEPTION AND CONTROL

Additional books in this series can be found on Nova's website under the Series tab.

Additional e-books in this series can be found on Nova's website under the e-book tab.

DRUG TRANSIT AND DISTRIBUTION, INTERCEPTION AND CONTROL

ILLEGAL DRUGS IN THE U.S.

MARKETS AND TRENDS FOR MARIJUANA, METH, HEROIN, AND COCAINE

LESLEY HARPER
EDITOR

nova publishers
New York

Copyright © 2014 by Nova Science Publishers, Inc.

All rights reserved. No part of this book may be reproduced, stored in a retrieval system or transmitted in any form or by any means: electronic, electrostatic, magnetic, tape, mechanical photocopying, recording or otherwise without the written permission of the Publisher.

For permission to use material from this book please contact us:
Telephone 631-231-7269; Fax 631-231-8175
Web Site: http://www.novapublishers.com

NOTICE TO THE READER

The Publisher has taken reasonable care in the preparation of this book, but makes no expressed or implied warranty of any kind and assumes no responsibility for any errors or omissions. No liability is assumed for incidental or consequential damages in connection with or arising out of information contained in this book. The Publisher shall not be liable for any special, consequential, or exemplary damages resulting, in whole or in part, from the readers' use of, or reliance upon, this material. Any parts of this book based on government reports are so indicated and copyright is claimed for those parts to the extent applicable to compilations of such works.

Independent verification should be sought for any data, advice or recommendations contained in this book. In addition, no responsibility is assumed by the publisher for any injury and/or damage to persons or property arising from any methods, products, instructions, ideas or otherwise contained in this publication.

This publication is designed to provide accurate and authoritative information with regard to the subject matter covered herein. It is sold with the clear understanding that the Publisher is not engaged in rendering legal or any other professional services. If legal or any other expert assistance is required, the services of a competent person should be sought. FROM A DECLARATION OF PARTICIPANTS JOINTLY ADOPTED BY A COMMITTEE OF THE AMERICAN BAR ASSOCIATION AND A COMMITTEE OF PUBLISHERS.

Additional color graphics may be available in the e-book version of this book.

Library of Congress Cataloging-in-Publication Data

ISBN: 978-1-63117-972-3

Published by Nova Science Publishers, Inc. † New York

CONTENTS

PREFACE

This book provides information on what America's users spend on illegal drugs and which markets have become larger. It also discusses what heroin, cocaine, methamphetamine, and marijuana are and the consequences of drug use.

Chapter 1 – A sense of scale is a prerequisite to thinking sensibly about illicit drug markets. For example, knowing whether a country consumes tens, hundreds, or thousands of metric tons (MTs) of a prohibited substance is critical for understanding the impact of a three-MT seizure at a border crossing. But decisionmakers need more than a sense of scale; they also need figures with enough precision to be able to determine whether the markets have become larger or smaller over time.

In January 2012, the U.S. White House Office of National Drug Control Policy (ONDCP) asked RAND Corporation to generate national estimates of the total number of users, total expenditures, and total consumption for four illicit drugs from 2000 to 2010: cocaine (including crack), heroin, marijuana, and methamphetamine (or meth). This report presents the results found and explains the methodology used.

Chapter 2 – This is a select material from Drugs of Abuse, Drugs of Abuse [Heroin, Cocaine, Methamphetamine, and Marijuana] by Drug Enforcement Agency) 2011 Edition.

In: Illegal Drugs in the U.S.
Editor: Lesley Harper
ISBN: 978-1-63117-972-3
© 2014 Nova Science Publishers, Inc.

Chapter 1

WHAT AMERICA'S USERS SPEND ON ILLEGAL DRUGS: 2000-2010*

B. Kilmer, S. Everingham, J. Caulkins, G. Midgette, R. Pacula, P. Reuter, R. Burns, B. Han and R. Lundberg

PREFACE

A sense of scale is a prerequisite to thinking sensibly about illicit drug markets. For example, knowing whether a country consumes tens, hundreds, or thousands of metric tons (MTs) of a prohibited substance is critical for understanding the impact of a three-MT seizure at a border crossing. But decisionmakers need more than a sense of scale; they also need figures with enough precision to be able to determine whether the markets have become larger or smaller over time.

In January 2012, the U.S. White House Office of National Drug Control Policy (ONDCP) asked RAND Corporation to generate national estimates of the total number of users, total expenditures, and total consumption for four illicit drugs from 2000 to 2010: cocaine (including crack), heroin, marijuana, and methamphetamine (or meth). This report presents the results found and explains the methodology used.

---

* This is an edited, reformatted and augmented version of a report prepared under federal contract for the Office of National Drug Control Policy, dated February 2014.

ABBREVIATIONS

ADAM	Arrestee Drug Abuse Monitoring Program
ADAM-I	Arrestee Drug Abuse Monitoring Program, ended in 2003
ADAM-II	Arrestee Drug Abuse Monitoring Program, 2007–10
CCDB	Consolidated Counterdrug Database
CDC	U.S. Centers for Disease Control and Prevention
CDU	chronic drug user
CMEA	Combat Methamphetamine Epidemic Act of 2005
CNC	Crime and Narcotics Center
DASC	Drug Availability Steering Committee
DAWN	Drug Abuse Warning Network
DEA	U.S. Drug Enforcement Agency
DMP	Domestic Monitoring Program
DSL	Domestic Super Lab
DTO	drug trafficking organizations
EQ	export quality
E/P	ephedrine/pseudoephedrine
EPH	ephedrine
FBI	Federal Bureau of Investigation
HSP	Heroin Signature Program
IACM	Interagency Assessment of Cocaine Movement
INCSR	*International Narcotics Control Strategy Report*
JIATF	Joint Interagency Task Force
MT	metric ton
MTF	Monitoring the Future
NESARC	U.S. National Epidemiologic Survey on Alcohol and Related Conditions
NHSDA	National Household Survey on Drug Abuse
NSDUH	National Survey on Drug Use and Health
NSS	National Seizure System
N-SSATS	National Survey of Substance Abuse Treatment Services
ONDCP	U.S. White House Office of National Drug Control Policy
P2P	phenyl-2-propanone method
PSE	pseudoephedrine
SAMHSA	Substance Abuse and Mental Health Services Administration
STL	Small Toxic Lab
STRIDE	System to Retrieve Information from Drug Evidence
TEDS	Treatment Episode Daily System

THC	tetrahydrocannabinol
UCR	Uniform Crime Reports
UNODC	United Nations Office on Drugs and Crime

EXECUTIVE SUMMARY

A sense of scale is a prerequisite to thinking sensibly about illicit drug markets. For example, knowing whether a country consumes tens, hundreds, or thousands of metric tons (MTs) of a prohibited substance is critical for understanding the impact of a three-MT seizure at a border crossing. But decisionmakers need more than a sense of scale; they also need figures with enough precision to be able to determine whether the markets have become larger or smaller over time.

In January 2012, the U.S. White House Office of National Drug Control Policy (ONDCP) asked RAND to generate national estimates of the total number of users, total expenditures, and total consumption for four illicit drugs from 2000 to 2010: cocaine (including crack), heroin, marijuana, and methamphetamine (or meth). This report explains our methodology and presents our results.

Among our main findings:

- Drug users in the United States spend on the order of $100 billion annually on cocaine, heroin, marijuana, and meth. While this total figure has been stable over the decade, there have been important compositional shifts. In 2000, much more money was spent on cocaine than marijuana; in 2010 the opposite was true.
- From 2002 to 2010, the amount of marijuana consumed in the United States likely increased by about 40 percent while the amount of cocaine consumed in the United States decreased by about 50 percent. These figures are consistent with supply-side indicators, such as seizures and production estimates.
- Heroin consumption remained fairly stable throughout the decade, although there is some evidence of an increase in the later years. Most of the heroin consumed in the United States comes from poppies grown in Colombia and Mexico, but data deficiencies surrounding associated production figures from 2005 to 2010 make comparisons difficult. There was a steady increase in the amount of heroin seized

within the United States and at the southwest border from 2007 through 2010.

- Methamphetamine estimates are subject to the greatest uncertainty because national datasets do not do a good job of capturing its use. Three particular challenges were that the Arrestee Drug Abuse Monitoring Program (ADAM-I) was discontinued in 2003, just before meth use was believed to be at its peak (2004–2006); ADAM-II did not start until 2007 (2007–2010) and it covers very few counties with substantial meth use; and the National Survey on Drug Use and Health (NSDUH) changed how it asked about meth use in 2007. While multiple indicators are consistent with an increasing trend in meth consumption over the first half of the decade and a subsequent decline through 2008, there is not comparable agreement as to the level. Further, we suggest that the most defensible position concerning trends from 2008 to 2010 is simply to admit the data are insufficient to provide clear guidance.
- For all of the drugs, total consumption and expenditures are driven by the minority of heavy users, who consume on 21 or more days each month.

Tables S.1.–S.3. present estimates of retail expenditures, chronic drug users (CDUs), and weight consumed, respectively. We present middle, lower, and higher estimates, as well as the figures published in the previous version of this series (which are only available through 2006; ONDCP, 2012c). The middle estimates could also be termed best estimates. The lower and higher ends of the range are meant to give some sense of the uncertainty, but they have a very specific and nuanced meaning that is vulnerable to misinterpretation. For cocaine, heroin, and meth, they reflect only one source of uncertainty: the 95-percent confidence interval surrounding the share of adult male arrest events involving a positive drug test. For marijuana expenditures and consumption, the lower estimate is based on NSDUH estimates with no adjustment for underreporting, and the higher estimate multiplies this value by two. Since there are many other sources of uncertainty, readers should not consider these as lower or upper bounds or as 95-percent confidence intervals. The range should be considered plausible, but not extreme.

Table S.1. Retail Expenditures on Illicit Drugs, 2000–2010 (in billions of 2010 dollars)

Drug	Estimate	2000	2001	2002	2003	2004	2005	2006	2007	2008	2009	2010
Cocaine	Middle	55	49	45	43	44	44	43	39	34	31	28
	Lower-Higher	37–83	33–73	30–69	28–67	29–69	28–68	28–65	25–59	22–51	20–48	18–44
	ONDCP (2012)	44	43	44	48	43	42	41				
Heroin	Middle	23	23	22	23	23	22	21	21	23	26	27
	Lower-Higher	12–40	12–39	12–37	12–37	12–37	12–35	11–35	12–35	12–37	14–44	15–45
	ONDCP (2012)	15	14	15	14	13	12	12				
Marijuana[a]	Middle	22	24	30	30	31	30	30	30	32	35	41
	Lower-Higher	14–28	16–32	21–43	22–44	23–45	22–44	22–44	22–44	23–46	26–53	30–60
	ONDCP (2012)	32	31	43	44	35	37	37				
Meth	Middle	8	11	15	17	20	23	22	20	16	15	13
	Lower-Higher	3–17	5–20	7–25	9–28	11–32	13–35	12–33	11–31	8–26	7–24	6–22
	ONDCP (2012)	15	14	15	16	18	19	19				
Total (All Four Drugs)	Middle	108	107	112	113	119	119	116	110	105	108	109
	ONDCP (2012)	106	102	117	122	109	110	109				

Notes: The lower and higher ends of the range are meant to give some sense of the uncertainty, but they have a very specific and nuanced meaning that is vulnerable to misinterpretation. Please see text.

[a] The 2000–2003 marijuana estimates are not perfectly comparable to the later years because of changes in survey questions and methods. These marijuana estimates are based on our "constant grams" series, which assumes that the amount of marijuana consumed in a use day did not change over the decade (meaning that average tetrahydrocannabinol (THC) consumption per use day increased). Our alternative "constant THC" series, which assumes that THC consumption per use day did not change (meaning that the average marijuana consumption per use day decreased), generates lower expenditure estimates that increase from $22 billion in 2000 to $26 billion in 2010 (in 2010 dollars).

Table S.2. Chronic Drug Users (Four or More Days in the Past Month), 2000–2010 (in millions)

Drug	Estimate	2000	2001	2002	2003	2004	2005	2006	2007	2008	2009	2010
Cocaine	Middle	3.3	3.1	2.9	2.9	3.1	3.2	3.2	3.0	2.8	2.7	2.5
	Lower–Higher	2.2–5.0	2.1–4.6	1.9–5.5	1.9–4.5	2.0–4.8	2.1–4.9	2.1-4.9	2.0–4.7	1.9–4.3	1.7–4.1	1.6–3.9
	ONDCP (2012)	2.6	2.7	2.6	2.8	2.8	2.8					
Heroin	Middle	1.4	1.4	1.3	1.3	1.3	1.3	1.2	1.2.	1.3	1.5	1.5
	Lower-Higher	0.7–2.4	0.7–2.4	0.7–2.2	0.7–2.1	0.7–2.1	0.7–2.0	0.7–2.0	0.7–2.0	0.7–2.2	0.8–2.5	0.8–2.6
	ONDCP (2012)	1.0	0.9	1.0	0.9	0.9	0.8	0.8				
Marijuana[a]	NSDUH-Adjusted	10.6	11.8	13.7	13.4	13.6	13.8	14.2	13.5	14.6	16.2	17.6
	NSDUH-Raw	7.0	7.9	10.0	9.8	9.9	10.2	10.5	9.9	10.6	12.0	12.9
	ONDCP (2012)	10.2	10.2	12.8	12.7	12.5	12.8	13.0				
Meth	Middle	0.9	1.2	1.6	1.9	2.2	2.6	2.6	2.3	2.0	1.8	1.6
	Lower-Higher	0.3–1.9	0.5–2.2	0.8–2.7	1.0–3.1	1.2–3.5	1.5–3.9	1.4–3.8	1.2–3.6	1.0–3.2	0.9–2.9	0.7–2.7
	ONDCP (2012)	0.8	0.9	0.9	1.0	1.2	1.3	1.3				

Notes: The lower and higher ends of the range are meant to give some sense of the uncertainty, but they have a very specific and nuanced meaning that is vulnerable to misinterpretation. Please see text.

[a] The 2000–2003 marijuana estimates are not perfectly comparable to the later years because of changes in survey questions and methods. NSDUH-Raw is based on the number of people reporting four or more days of marijuana use in the past month. NSDUH-Adjusted inflates the NSDUH-Raw figures to account for survey undercounting.

The biggest discrepancy between the current estimates and what was previously published is with respect to consumption (Table S.3.), and this is largely driven by how the retail price is estimated. The modal retail purchase that arrestees report for cocaine powder, crack, heroin, and meth is only $20. Retail price trends for these substances are customarily monitored at the level of one (pure) gram, which is a much larger purchase. Since illegal drugs are subject to very considerable quantity discounts, gram-level prices are not a good reflection of the average amount that heavy users spend per pure gram obtained. We generate new price series with lower "referent quantities" that are closer to the quantity typically purchased in a street-level sale. These new price series suggest users are paying more per pure gram obtained, and so are consuming less per dollar spent, than would have been presumed in the past.

Table S.3. Consumption of Illicit Drugs, 2000–2010 (in pure metric tons, except marijuana)

Drug	Estimate	2000	2001	2002	2003	2004	2005	2006	2007	2008	2009	2010
Cocaine	Middle	292	258	278	278	324	327	322	282	200	161	145
	Lower-Higher	193–440	175°386	183–428	182–428	209–500	211–501	208–494	182–431	132–302	105–248	92–227
	ONDCP (2012)	255	228	253	337	346	372	390				
Drug	Estimate	2000	2001	2002	2003	2004	2005	2006	2007	2008	2009	2010
Heroin	Middle	22	25	22	23	23	22	22	24	26	27	24
	Lower-Higher	11–37	13–41	12–37	12–38	12–37	12–36	12–36	13–39	14–42	15–45	13–40
	ONDCP (2012)	32	31	33	32	29	27	28				
Marijuana[a] (1,000 MTs)	Middle	3.0	3.5	4.0	4.0	4.2	4.1	4.3	4.3	4.7	5.1	5.7
	Lower-Higher	2.0–3.9	2.3–4.7	2.9–5.7	2.9–5.8	3.0–6.1	3.1–6.1	3.1–6.2	3.1–6.2	3.4–6.8	3.8–7.5	4.2–8.4
	ONDCP (2012)	4.6	4.6	4.5	5.1	5.2	4.8	4.3				
Meth	Middle	20	26	41	48	61	85	58	54	39	40	42
	Lower-Higher	8–43	11–49	20–70	24–77	32–95	47–127	32–88	28–83	20–63	19–66	19–71
	ONDCP (2012)	66	72	89	118	143	167	157				

Notes: The lower and higher ends of the range are meant to give some sense of the uncertainty, but they have a very specific and nuanced meaning that is vulnerable to misinterpretation. Please see text.

[a] The 2000–2003 marijuana estimates are not perfectly comparable to the later years because of changes in survey questions and methods.

There is great uncertainty surrounding these market-size estimates, particularly for methamphetamine. In many cases, the extent of the uncertainty cannot be bounded or quantified. Though this analysis weaves together information from a variety of indicators, survey self-reports remain a principal source of information about user behaviors—frequency, quantity, and spending. The organizations conducting these surveys expend considerable effort trying to minimize misreporting, including sometimes confirming self-reported data by testing users for the presence of drugs. Nevertheless, there is no way to entirely escape the basic limitations of survey self-reporting, and unfortunately supply-side estimates are plagued by different but equally severe limitations.

Can these demand-side estimates for illicit drugs be improved? The answer depends on the drug. In brief, we are optimistic about the possibility of refining the marijuana estimates. In contrast, we are decidedly pessimistic about meth, for which much of the use falls outside the ambit of the standard data systems. The prospect of improving estimates of the size of cocaine and heroin markets largely depends on whether the surveys that reach heavy users of these two drugs could be enhanced and extended.

1. Illicit Drug Market Estimation

1.1. Introduction

A sense of scale is a prerequisite to thinking sensibly about illicit drug markets. For example, knowing whether a country consumes tens, hundreds, or thousands of metric tons (MTs) of a prohibited substance is critical for understanding the impact of a three-MT seizure at a border crossing. But decisionmakers need more than a sense of scale; they also need figures with enough precision to be able to determine whether the markets have gotten larger or smaller over time.

Estimating the size of illicit drug markets—whether it be in terms of users, expenditures, or quantity consumed—is a difficult task. The difficulty is not conceptual; at root, it is just counting. The problem is largely with the data. That statement is in no way a criticism of those who design and administer the data systems upon which we rely. Rather, it is an inevitable consequence of trying to measure sales of something sold in hidden markets or consumption behavior that is both illegal and dominated by a relatively small number of heavy users.

One corollary is that this task involves a lot of uncertainty. Depending on the substance and the construct being measured, determining the direction of trends may be the best that can be done. Numbers of chronic users can be estimated more accurately than spending, which in turn is subject to less uncertainty than estimates of quantities (weights) consumed.

Likewise, there is a stronger evidentiary foundation for marijuana (due to its higher prevalence) than for cocaine, and stronger evidence for cocaine than for heroin or methamphetamine. Were someone to trumpet estimates of the latter quantities as having narrow error bands, those claims should be met with great skepticism.

A second corollary is that the task requires judgment. Most of the uncertainty does not come from sampling variability, for which one can compute statistical confidence intervals. Instead, it comes from questions about the raw data, such as the extent to which one can trust arrestees' self-reports about their spending on illegal drugs, and how to extrapolate just ten urban areas' arrest records to the country as a whole—particularly for a drug like meth, for which the user base appears not to be concentrated in large cities.

There is an emerging scientific literature on sizing illicit drug markets, mostly in developed countries. Pioneering work for the United States has been conducted by Abt Associates, under contract for the U.S. White House Office of National Drug Control Policy (ONDCP). Those reports (Rhodes, Langenbahn, Kling, & Scheiman, 1997; ONDCP, 1991; 2001; 2012c) provide a strong foundation and their methodologies have evolved over time as data systems have improved. Much of the non-U.S. work on sizing drug markets focuses on cannabis (e.g., Wilkins, Reilly, Pledger, & Casswell, 2005; Bouchard, 2007; van Laar, Frijns, Trautmann, & Lombi, 2013), although some analyses address other drugs (e.g., Pudney et al., 2006; Vopravil & Běláčková, 2012; European Monitoring Centre for Drugs and Drug Addiction, 2013; Kilmer et al., 2013b).[1] In January 2012, ONDCP asked RAND to generate national estimates of the total number of chronic users, total expenditures, and total consumption for four drugs from 2000 through 2010: cocaine (including crack), heroin, marijuana, and meth.[2]

The rest of this Section describes different approaches for estimating the size of illicit markets. They fall into two general categories: supply side and demand side.

We discuss their strengths and weaknesses, and highlight that different approaches may be better suited for different substances. These supply-side and demand-side approaches often yield different results and we note this phenomenon is not specific to illicit drugs. The Section concludes with a road map for the report and highlights its innovations and contributions.

1.2. Drug Market Estimation Strategies

There are four general approaches for estimating the size of an illicit drug market.[3] On the supply side, there are production-based and seizure-based estimates; on the demand side, there are consumption-based and expenditure-based estimates.[4] Their contrasting strengths and weaknesses play out differently for different substances, making it important to choose the right combination of methods for each drug.

1.2.1. Supply-Side Estimation Strategies

Production-based estimates for organically–based drugs typically start with information about the amount of land under cultivation, drawn from aerial or satellite imagery and interviews with farmers.[5] After accounting for eradication efforts, various factors (e.g., leaf yield, alkaloid content, processing efficiency for cocaine, dry weight per unit harvested) are used to develop a purity-adjusted potential production estimate. Multipliers reflecting the fraction of product that is successfully passed to each subsequent stage of the delivery chain are applied to generate an estimate of the drug available in the user country. These results are highly sensitive to yield estimates based on field research, which vary across time and by location.

Seizure-based estimates divide the quantity of drugs that are seized or eradicated by the proportion of drugs that are believed to be seized or eradicated. An obvious concern with this method is that the proportion of drugs that are seized or eradicated is unknown. Seizures are not necessarily proportional to the drug flow and often depend on law enforcement efforts and countermeasures taken by drug traffickers (Reuter, 1995).

1.2.2. Demand-Side Estimation Strategies

Consumption-based estimates typically multiply the number of users by the product of days of use per month or year ("use days") and grams consumed per use day. This number is computed separately for users of different intensities and then summed (weighting by the numbers of each type of user) to obtain the overall market estimate. The first two values (number of users and use days) are usually available from government-sponsored surveys or treatment intake assessments; caveated as always by the limits of asking individuals to accurately and honestly self-report illegal activities, and the possibility that changing attitudes might influence reporting rates (which might exaggerate year-to-year changes). The third value, grams consumed per use day, is much harder to come by. Most large surveys do not inquire about this, and few respondents know the precise weight of what they consume.

Expenditure-based estimates combine user counts with estimates of the amount ***spent*** on drugs, rather than amounts ***consumed***. An advantage of this approach is that although users generally do not know the exact quantity of drug that they bought, let alone its purity or potency, they often know how much they spent on it. These data are then combined with (purity-adjusted) price per unit weight to generate an estimate of the weight consumed. Beyond getting good information about heavy users (which is also an issue for consumption-based estimates), a challenge to this approach is obtaining the necessary information about purity-adjusted prices. While information about the price per pure gram is becoming increasingly available (Caulkins, Pacula, et al., 2004; Fries, Anthony, Cseko, et al., 2008; ONDCP, 2013a), most users do not purchase in units of pure grams; retail transactions of the big three expensive drugs (cocaine, heroin, and meth) are usually smaller, and never at 100-percent purity. This requires making additional adjustments to account for quantity discounts obtained over the distribution of retail purchase sizes (Caulkins & Padman, 1993).

1.2.3. Which Strategy Should Be Used for Which Drugs?

The best strategy for generating consumption estimates for specific drugs will largely depend on the available data, where the drug is produced, and the size of the market being considered. For example, available evidence suggests that most of the cocaine consumed in the United States is from coca cultivated in Colombia (U.S. Drug Enforcement Agency [DEA], 2003; United Nations Office on Drugs and Crime [UNODC], 2011). Since the U.S. Federal Government and UNODC both estimate the amount of land dedicated to coca production as well as yield per hectare, the production-based approach is a good place to start for understanding U.S. cocaine consumption. On the other hand, marijuana consumed in the United States is both produced domestically and imported from Mexico and other countries. Since we do not have marijuana production estimates for the United States and the pre-2011 estimates of Mexican marijuana production are no longer believed to be reliable (see Section Seven), a demand-based approach is preferred for estimating marijuana consumption.

Given the limits associated with all of these strategies, it is useful where possible to produce multiple independent estimates and see if they agree. For this report, RAND was asked to generate demand-side estimates that could be compared with supply-side indicators (which we do in Section Seven). There is a tendency for "top-down" supply-side approaches to differ from "bottom-up" demand-side estimates, but this does not mean it is appropriate to simply combine the estimates and consider the midpoint the best. Care must be taken to understand the limits of the underlying data and how these limits are addressed.

Indeed, this supply versus demand gap is not specific to illicit drugs. Much more work has been done on estimating quantities consumed of tobacco and alcohol, and some studies have compared these figures with "official" supply-side estimates (e.g., information based on excise taxes and sales receipts). An international literature review suggests it is reasonable to assume that general population surveys underestimate alcohol consumption, sometimes by more than 50 percent (Gmel and Rehm, 2004).[6] Similarly, Cook (2007) compared self-report data from the U.S. National Epidemiologic Survey on Alcohol and Related Conditions (NESARC) with alcohol sales information and found that NESARC "provides an estimate of per capita consumption that is about half of recorded per capita sales."

Likewise, a study that compared cigarette consumption in the U.S. general population with estimates from the Federal Trade Commission and other sources suggested that underreporting ranged from 10 percent to 40 percent (ONDCP, 2012c). This same study also found that demand-side alcohol estimates can either account for less than half of supply-side estimates or approximate them reasonably well, depending on the source of the official supply statistics. One response to the data limitations is to keep the methods straightforward and transparent. Straightforward is not the same as simple. The bridge constructed from the raw data to the final estimates involves many steps, some of which are technical in the sense of responding to idiosyncrasies of drug use and drug markets. However, this report strives to make the logic and the limitations of each of the many steps clear to any analyst well-versed in this domain.

1.3. How This Report Contributes to the Science of Illicit Drug Market Estimation

Our expenditure and consumption estimates of cocaine, heroin, marijuana, and meth are based on a demand-side approach that begins by calculating the number of chronic users. For all four substances, the estimates draw on the complementary strengths of the National Survey on Drug Use and Health (NSDUH) and the Arrestee Drug Abuse Monitoring Program (ADAM), supplemented by a wide range of other data sources; however, the approach for marijuana differs from what is used for the other substances. To simplify, the approach used for estimating marijuana users is rooted in the general population survey (NSDUH), then augmented with additional information on arrestees (ADAM) and youth (Monitoring the Future [MTF] program). For cocaine, heroin, and methamphetamine, the opposite approach is taken: Estimates are rooted in ADAM and then supplemented with NSDUH and other sources.

NSDUH does a good job of collecting information for a large share of chronic marijuana users; however, this is not the case for the big three "expensive" drugs. For cocaine, heroin, and meth, it makes sense to start with a database of arrestees because chronic users of these substances are often involved with the criminal justice system. They are less likely to show up in general population studies, either because they are literally outside the household population or because of nonresponse and underreporting by those who are theoretically within NSDUH's sampling frame (ONDCP, 2012c).

This analysis benefits from a foundation established by Abt's previous work in this series (Rhodes et al., 1997; ONDCP, 1991; 2001; 2012c). However, our approach extends and refines previous approaches in the following ways:

- **It distinguishes among four different types of drug users**. Previous efforts have generally focused on just two types of users: those using on four or more days in the past month (termed "chronic users") and those using less often (termed "occasional users"). Differentiating between more and less frequent users is crucial because frequent users consume so much more per capita. However, since the last report in this series, it has become increasingly clear that consumption rates are even skewed within chronic users, not just between chronic and less frequent users: Daily/near-daily users have strikingly different consumption patterns than those who use weekly or even several times a week. It is the daily/ near-daily users in particular who drive consumption. Hence, the estimates here differentiate among three types of chronic users: daily/near-daily (21 or more times in the past month), more than weekly (11–20 times in the past month), weekly (four to ten times in the past month). They also count those using less than four times in the past month, but this group consumes so much less per capita than the others that it contributes very little to total spending or use.

- **We use ADAM data to estimate proportions instead of counts.** While an integral part of the analysis, ADAM-I (discontinued in 2003) and ADAM-II (2007–10) data are erratic, both in the sense of varying in inexplicable ways over time in certain counties and in the sense of not always mirroring trends in other indicators. Some of these irregularities can be pinned on problems with sampling weights, but puzzles remain even for the subset of locations and years for which the newer, improved weights are available. For reasons elaborated in the Technical Report, we believe this makes ADAM stronger for estimating a proportion— specifically the proportion of arrestees testing positive—than a count. This approach is inspired by work done by Brecht et al. (2008).
- **We recognize that frequent users often do not receive quantity discounts.** Heavy users of expensive drugs are often impoverished and unable to maintain large inventories of either cash or drugs; thus, the modal retail purchase arrestees report for cocaine powder, crack, heroin, and meth is only \$20. Retail price trends for these substances are customarily monitored at the level of one (pure) gram, which is a much larger purchase.
  Since illegal drugs are subject to considerable quantity discounts, gram-level prices are not a good reflection of the average amount that heavy users spend per pure gram obtained. We generate a new price series from the DEA's System to Retrieve Information from Drug Evidence (STRIDE) data with lower "referent quantities" that are closer to the quantity (in pure grams) typically purchased for each drug in a street-level sale. These new price series suggest users are paying more per pure gram obtained and so are consuming less per dollar spent than would have been presumed in the past.
- **We acknowledge the possible nonrepresentativeness of most recent marijuana purchases.** Over a decade ago the Substance Abuse and Mental Health Services Administration (SAMHSA) added questions to NSDUH about the most recent marijuana purchase. These questions have been enormously useful to researchers, but multiplying the number of purchases in a given period by the amount spent on the most recent purchase may not provide a reasonable estimate of total marijuana spending. It would—***only*** if the most recent purchase was representative of all purchases. If larger purchases are followed by longer gaps before the next subsequent purchase, then those larger purchases would be oversampled by

surveys administered at random times, which would tend to overestimate spending. The extent of upward bias can be very large if individuals do not always purchase a standard amount, and is very hard to bound. Thus, we use a different approach that avoids making this untestable and possibly unwarranted assumption.

- **Our approach incorporates marijuana potency trends into the expenditure estimates.** THC is the primary intoxicant in marijuana. THC levels increased substantially from 2000 to 2010 not only because higher potency marijuana gained market share relative to lower-potency commercial-grade, but also because the potency of commercial-grade marijuana grew. Since prices unadjusted for potency seem to have been fairly stable over the decade (possibly even decreasing after adjusting for inflation), consumers now pay less to achieve the same level of intoxication.
- **We use additional data sources to generate estimates of the number of chronic drug users (CDUs).** This analysis uses data from ADAM-I and ADAM-II, where previous analyses were limited to data from ADAM-I.

  Although smaller in sites and samples, ADAM-II is critical for helping understand trends throughout the decade. These analyses also incorporate a number of state- and substate-level market demand indicators that were not used in previous efforts, including drug-specific mortality rates and drug test results from employers.

The rest of the report is organized as follows. Section Two describes our estimates of the number of users for the three "expensive" drugs (cocaine, heroin, and meth) while Sections Three and Four address expenditures and the total weight consumed, respectively.

Section Five focuses on sizing the national marijuana market. Section Six examines the issue of polydrug use (we found there is generally little overlap among chronic users of the expensive drugs).

Section Seven compares our consumption estimates with supply-side indicators, including production estimates and seizure statistics. Section Eight concludes with some thoughts for further improving illicit drug market estimation.

2. Estimating the Number of Chronic Cocaine, Heroin, and Methamphetamine Users

2.1. Introduction

This section presents annual estimates of the number of chronic cocaine, heroin, and methamphetamine users in the United States for 2000–2010. To remain consistent with previous studies in this series, we define a chronic user as someone who used a particular drug on four or more days in the previous month. Hence, "chronic" is defined in terms of current frequency of use, not duration of use. Also, if someone used cocaine on three days and heroin on three other days in the previous month (i.e., six days of hard-drug use in the previous month), they would not meet this definition of chronic user.[7]

Our approach is rooted in ADAM and builds on prior work, including previous efforts to estimate CDUs (e.g., Brecht et al., 2003; ONDCP, 2001; 2012c). ADAM's advantages are clear; it includes an objective measure of substance use (urinalysis) not just self-report, and it captures chronic users—who are responsible for the great bulk of consumption—far better than other surveys (ONDCP 2012c). Its principal limitation for estimating the number of CDUs in the nation is also clear; ADAM is not nationally representative. Indeed, since the end of ADAM-I in 2003, its coverage is quite limited. The program did not collect data from 2004 to 2006, and was brought back in just ten counties from 2007 to 2010 (in 2011 it dropped to five counties). Hence, we supplement ADAM with other datasets that provide insights about drug consumption at the state and county levels, and doing so requires using a different estimation methodology than had been used with ADAM in the past.

A detailed description of our methodology and how it compared to the previous report (ONDCP, 2012c) is provided in the accompanying Technical Report. This Section gives an overview of our approach and presents estimates of the number of CDUs of cocaine, heroin, and meth for 2000– 2010.

2.2. Methodology

Our approach involves eight major steps that are implemented separately for cocaine, heroin, and meth, where cocaine should be understood to mean cocaine in any form, including both powder and crack.

Step 1. Quantify the relationship between the share of positive drug tests among adult male arrest events in ADAM jurisdictions and county and state-level covariates that are available for all counties in the country.

Step 2. Project the share of positive drug tests among adult male arrest events in all counties using the model generated in Step 1.

Step 3. For counties with reliable Uniform Crime Reports UCR arrest data, multiply this predicted rate by the number of adult male arrest events. This generates an estimate of the number of male arrest events that involve someone who would test positive.

Step 4. Sum across these counties and scale up using UCR national estimates to project the national total of adult male arrest events involving someone who would test positive.

Step 5. Convert the number of adult male arrest events involving someone who would test positive to adult male arrest events involving a CDU.

Step 6. Convert the total number of adult male arrest ***events*** involving a CDU to the total of adult male ***arrestees*** who were CDUs (i.e., from events to individuals).

Step 7. Inflate the total of adult male arrestees who were CDUs to the total of adult male CDUs (i.e., include both those who were criminally active but happened to not get arrested in the last year and those who were not criminally active apart from their drug use).

Step 8. Adjust the national total of adult male CDUs to account for females and juveniles.

Each of these steps involves a number of substeps that are described in the accompanying Technical Report. The remainder of this section presents an overview of our approach, grouping Steps 1–4 and Steps 5–8.

2.2.1. Steps 1-4: National Total of Adult Male Arrest Events Involving Someone Who Would Test Positive

Our main task is to take drug use levels among arrestees in ADAM counties and relate them to state and substate variables that are available for all (or substantially all) counties in the country, not just for ADAM counties. That relationship can then be used to estimate levels of drug use among arrestees in counties for which ADAM data are not collected. For example, we would expect the proportion of arrestees testing positive for cocaine to be higher in counties with greater overall prevalence of cocaine, greater demand for cocaine treatment, more job applicants testing positive for cocaine, and more cocaine overdose events. So, in non-ADAM counties with high rates of those predictors, our model would predict that a high proportion of arrestees would have tested positive if ADAM and its urinalysis monitoring had been implemented in the county.

Table 2.1 lists the data sources used in the prediction models as well as the model-fit statistics for the preferred specifications. The accompanying Technical Report includes detailed information about these sources, estimated parameters, and the process used for selecting a preferred model.

Table 2.1. Covariates Used to Predict Drug Prevalence Rates

		Cocaine	Opiates	Meth
Socioeconomic	Population	X	X	X
	Poverty rate	X	X	X
	High school graduation rate	X	X	X
	Percent of population ages 18–24	X	X	X
NSDUH	State			X
	Substate	X		
Treatment	Treatment Episode Daily System (TEDS)—Cocaine	X	X	X
	TEDS—Heroin	X	X	X
	TEDS—Meth	X	X	X
	N-SSATS-Methadone		X	
QUEST	Positive test rate for cocaine	X	X	X
CDC	Cocaine mortality	X	X	X
	Heroin mortality		X	
	Psychostimulants mortality	X	X	
	Model-fit statistics for preferred specification			
	Observations	183	183	183
	R2	0.899	0.733	0.822
	Akaike information criterion	45.08	219.1	315.2
	Bayesian information criterion	199.1	299.2	379.4
	Number of covariates	47	24	19

Notes: Region-fixed effects were included in all models. Time and interaction effects were handled differently for each drug, which explains the different number of covariates for each model. See Technical Report for more information.

Having determined the best-performing model for each drug, we used that model to predict county-year positive rates for the ADAM and non-ADAM counties based on their observed values for the covariates in each drug's model. This generated a predicted value for each county-year as well as 95-percent confidence intervals for these estimates.

Table 2.2. Estimating the Number of Chronic Hard-Drug Users (four or more days in the past month)

Factor	Adjustments	Data	Years covered	For which user categories?
Start: Number of adult male arrest events with a positive urinalysis test				
F1	1. For adult male arrest events with a positive test, percent using four or more days in past montha	ADAM-II (based information) on urinalysis and self-report	Average across annual estimates, 2000–03, 2007–10	Calculate for three groups: four to ten use days in past month, 11–20 days, 21 or more days
Multiplying by F1 yields the number of adult male CDU arrest events with a positive urinalysis test				
F2	2. Number of arrests with positive test per person arrested and testing positivea	ADAM-I-II (based on self-report information about arrests in the past year, excluding warrants)	Estimate from pooled ADAM-I-II (2000–03, 2007–10)	Calculate for two groups: four to ten use days in past month, 11 or more daysb
Dividing by F2 yields the number of adult male CDUs who are arrested and have a positive urinalysis test				
F3	3. Proportion of adult male criminally active CDUs who get arrested each year a	Take arrests per arrestee from #2, assumes criminally active CDUs get arrested according to a Poisson distributionc	Estimate from pooled ADAM-I-II (2000–03, 2007–10)	Calculate for two groups four to ten use days in past month, 11 or more daysb
Dividing by F3 yields active adult male CDUs the number of criminally				
F4	4. Adult male CDUs who are not criminally active	Number of adult male CDUs who report never having been arrested in NSDUH, multiplied by 4d	Estimate from pooled NSDUH (2000–10)	Calculate for three groups: four to ten use days in past month, 11–20 days, 21 or more days

Table 2.2. (Continued)

Factor	Adjustments	Data	Years covered	For which user categories?
Adding F4 gives the number of adult male CDUs				
F5	5. Ratio of adult CDUs (male + female) to just adult male CDUs	Drug-specific ratios from (1) NSDUH Days of Use, (2) NSDUH CDUs Days of Use, (3) NSDUH number of CDUs, (4) TEDS Users in Treatment, (5) TEDS CDUs in Treatment, (6) Drug Abuse Warning Network (DAWN), (7) Vital Stats overdoses	Generate 2000–2010 average for each of these seven factors, take simple average of these seven values	Calculated for one group: four or more days in past month
Multiplying by F5 gives the number of adult CDUs				
F6	6. Ratio of all CDUs (adult + juvenile) to just adult CDUs	Drug-specific ratios from 1) NSDUH Days of Use, 2) NSDUH CDUs Days of Use, 3) NSDUH number of CDUs, 4) TEDS Users in Treatment, 5) TEDS CDUs in Treatment	Generate annual average across these five factors, impose linear trend for cocaine and meth (heroin constant 0.03)	Calculated for one group: four or more days in past month
Multiplying by F6 gives the number of CDUs				

[a] ADAM-I-II: No weights, do not account for those who refuse urinalysis test, no data for 2004–2006.

[b] To boost sample, combine those who used on 11–20 days with those who used 21 or more days. Dropping those brought in on warrants has relatively little effect.

[c] Different from ONDCP (2012c) because we use Poisson assumption only to extrapolate to criminally active CDUs who did not get arrested, not to all CDU who do not get arrested.

[d] Based on ONDCP (2012c) assumption that occasional users of cocaine, heroin, and meth in NSDUH should be multiplied by four because of underreporting.

We then multiplied these county-specific rates by the number of adult male arrests in each county for counties that consistently submit reliable arrest information for the Federal Bureau of Investigation (FBI) Uniform Crime Reports.[8.] We then scale our estimates from counties with high reporting rates to the entire nation using the ratio of total national UCR arrests to those for the consistently reporting counties. This generates annual estimates for male arrest events involving an arrestee who is projected to test positive for cocaine, opiates, or methamphetamine.

2.2.2. Steps 5-8: Moving from Predicted Positive Tests to the National Number of Chronic Drug Users

Moving from the predicted number of adult male arrest events with a positive test in the country to the national number of CDUs requires making a number of adjustments. Table 2.2 describes these adjustments and the data sources consulted. All of the adjustments are drug-specific. When possible they are done separately for three types of chronic drug users: those who used that particular drug four to ten days in the previous month, those who used 11–20 days in the previous month, and those who used 21 or more days in the previous month. Since the last report in this series (ONDCP, 2012c), it has become increasingly clear that consumption rates are even skewed within chronic users, not just between chronic and less-frequent users; daily/near-daily users (21 or more days) have strikingly different consumption patterns than those who use weekly or even several times a week. It is the daily/near-daily users who account for most of the consumption, not chronic users overall. The Technical Report includes detailed descriptions of each adjustment. The adjustments moving from arrest events with a positive test to adult male arrestees who are CDUs (factors F1 and F2 in Table 2.2) are based on ADAM and are fairly straightforward. Similarly, moving from the total number of adult male CDUs to a national estimate of all CDUs (F5 and F6 in Table 2.2) involves making adjustments to include females and juveniles that are based on insights from NSDUH, the TEDS, DAWN, and mortality data.

The middle adjustments that move from adult male CDUs who have been arrested to all adult male CDUs (F4 and F5 in Table 2.2) require more explanation. After converting from total male arrest events involving a CDU to adult male CDUs who were arrested (i.e., from events to people), we supplement this with an estimate of adult male CDUs who were criminally active but who happened to avoid arrest. In particular, dividing the number of CDUs arrested by the probability a CDU is arrested in a given year inflates the count to include those who happened not to have been arrested. This adjustment has similar logic to what was done in the previous version of this report (ONDCP, 2012c), but is different because we use a Poisson assumption only to extrapolate to criminally active CDUs who did not get arrested.

We then make a final adjustment to account for CDUs who had minimal risk of arrest. Of course all CDUs are at some risk of arrest because, by definition, they are using illegal drugs. Practically speaking, however, people who commit no offense other than drug use and who both purchase and consume inside a private residence, not in public, may be at very little risk of arrest. We estimate the size of this population that is hidden from arrestee surveys using NSDUH. Our (imperfect) proxy for a CDU being at negligible risk of arrest is never having been arrested at all, not just having avoided arrest in the last 12 months. Since NSDUH misses a lot of hard-drug users, we follow the previous report's adjustments for occasional drug users in NSDUH and multiply this population by four. Adding this to the CDU total generates an estimate the number of adults male CDUs in the country.

2.3. Results

2.3.1. Cocaine

Figure 2.1 presents the middle or "point" estimates of the number of chronic cocaine users (i.e., those who used on four or more days in the previous month) surrounded by an error band. The point estimate decreased from 3.3 million in 2000 to 2.5 million in 2010. The error band in this figure reflects only one source of uncertainty: The 95-percent confidence interval surrounding the share of adult male arrest events involving a positive drug test for cocaine. There are many other sources of uncertainty, but those other sources of uncertainty do not stem from sampling variability and so do not lend themselves to quantification. Thus, readers should not consider these as lower or upper bounds or as a 95-percent confidence interval for the number of chronic cocaine users.

Given the width of the error band, the middle estimate is entirely consistent with the cocaine CDU figures published in the previous version of this report (ONDCP, 2012c); both suggest that the number of chronic cocaine users from 2000–2006 was on the order of 3 million. After 2006, there is a steady decrease through 2010, with the latter being about 20 percent lower.

Since these CDU estimates draw on several data sources (not only ADAM but also self-reported past-month use from the NSDUH household survey, treatment admissions in TEDS, etc.), we would expect to see similar trends in some, if not most, of these series as well.

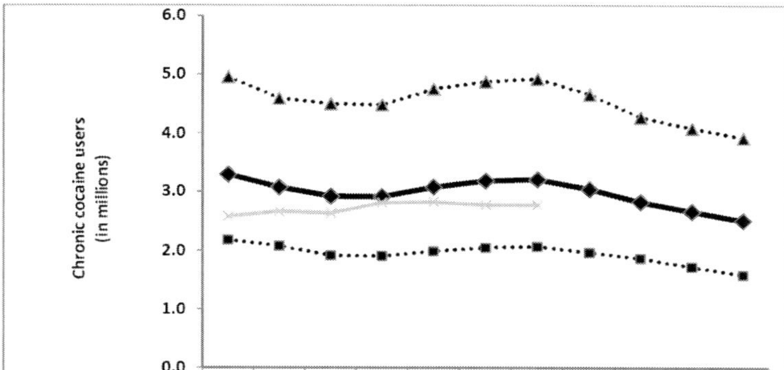

	2000	2001	2002	2003	2004	2005	2006	2007	2008	2009	2010
Middle	3.3	3.1	2.9	2.9	3.1	3.2	3.2	3.0	2.8	2.7	2.5
Lower	2.2	2.1	1.9	1.9	2.0	2.1	2.1	2.0	1.9	1.7	1.6
Higher	5.0	4.6	4.5	4.5	4.8	4.9	4.9	4.7	4.3	4.1	3.9
ONDCP (2012)	2.6	2.7	2.6	2.8	2.8	2.8	2.8				

Note: Lower and higher estimates have a very specific and nuanced meaning that is vulnerable to misinterpretation; please see accompanying text in Section 2.3.1.

Figure 2.1. Estimated Number of Chronic Cocaine Users, 2000–2010 (In Millions).

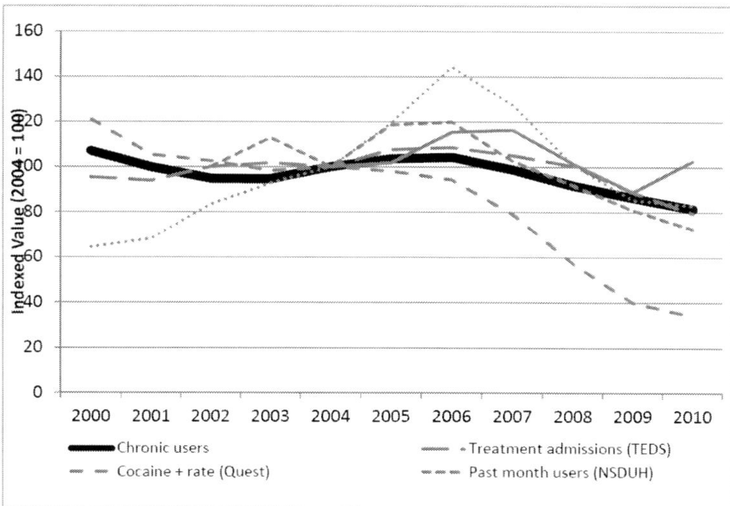

Figure 2.2. Comparison of Indexed National Cocaine Use Series, 2000–2010 (100 = 2004 Value).

Figure 2.2 displays the data (scaled to have a value of 100 in 2004) and all of the sources do show a large decline after 2006.[9] It also displays national estimates of emergency department visits involving cocaine from DAWN (not included in our model), which show a decline from 2006 to 2009, but then a slight increase from 2009 to 2010.

Although not directly comparable, this decrease is also consistent with drug testing data from the Department of Defense (which were not used for this analysis). Among positive drug test results for members of the military, the share attributable to cocaine decreased from 28.2 percent in fiscal year 2007 to 13.2 percent in fiscal year 2010.

Table 2.3 breaks down the estimated number of chronic cocaine users by frequency of use: four to ten days in the past month, 11–20 days, and 21 or more days. The 11–20 group is slightly smaller than the 21-days-or-more group, which is about half the size of the four-to-ten-days group.

Table 2.3. Millions of Chronic Cocaine Users by Frequency, 2000–2010

	2000	2001	2002	2003	2004	2005	2006	2007	2008	2009	2010
21+ days in past month	0.9	0.8	0.8	0.8	0.8	0.9	0.9	0.8	0.8	0.7	0.6
11–20 days in past month	0.7	0.6	0.6	0.6	0.6	0.7	0.7	0.6	0.6	0.6	0.5
4–10 days in past month	1.7	1.6	1.5	1.5	1.6	1.6	1.7	1.6	1.5	1.4	1.3

Note: Figure 2.1 displays some of the uncertainty surrounding these CDU estimates. Since the distribution of CDUs is similar for ADAM-I (2000–2003) and ADAM-II (2007–2010), we average these figures and apply the same ratio to all years (39 percent, 23 percent, 38 percent). Thus, these three groups all display the same trends.

2.3.2. Heroin

Figure 2.3 presents estimates of the number of chronic heroin users. The point estimates increased slightly from 1.4 million in 2000 to 1.5 million in 2010, but given the width of the error band, that is essentially no change. Similar to Figure 2.1, the error band presented is only driven by one source of uncertainty: the 95-percent confidence interval surrounding the predicted share of adult male arrest events involving a positive drug test for opiates.

Similar to the previous report (ONDCP, 2012c), our heroin estimates did not change much from 2000 to 2006. Both suggest a slight downward trend, but given the large error band we cannot say anything definitive about this change. There is, however, an important difference in terms of levels: Our CDU estimates are about 45 percent larger.[10] Since the number of heroin CDUs is much smaller than the number of cocaine CDUs (especially true earlier in the decade), it is more difficult to precisely estimate the former. Indeed, our error bands are larger for heroin than for cocaine. Given the greater uncertainty and our use of different methods and data sources, we are not surprised that our CDU estimates are less similar for heroin than they are for cocaine.

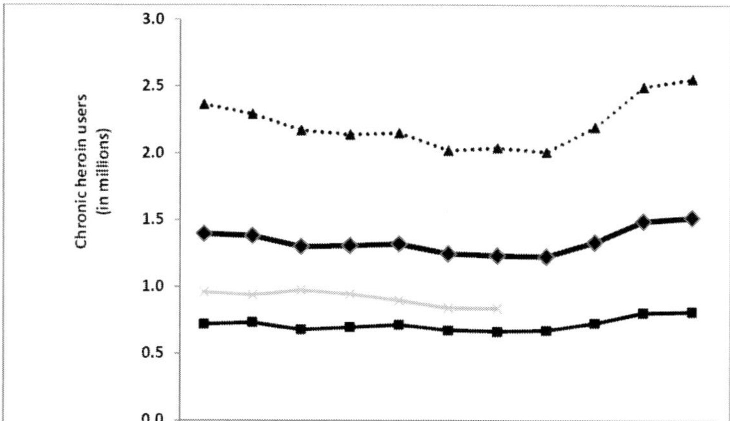

	2000	2001	2002	2003	2004	2005	2006	2007	2008	2009	2010
Middle	1.4	1.4	1.3	1.3	1.3	1.2	1.2	1.2	1.3	1.5	1.5
Lower	0.7	0.7	0.7	0.7	0.7	0.7	0.7	0.7	0.7	0.8	0.8
Higher	2.4	2.3	2.2	2.1	2.1	2.0	2.0	2.0	2.2	2.5	2.6
ONDCP (2012)	1.0	0.9	1.0	0.9	0.9	0.8	0.8				

Note: Lower and higher estimates have a very specific and nuanced meaning that is vulnerable to misinterpretation; please see accompanying text in Section 2.3.1.

Figure 2.3. Estimated Number of Chronic Heroin Users, 2000–2010 (In Millions).

The slight decline appears to stop in 2007 and is followed by a nearly 25-percent increase in heroin CDUs from 2007 to 2010.[11] We do not want to read too much into this given the large amount of uncertainty, but it is consistent with anecdotal reports about prescription opiates becoming a "gateway drug" to heroin for some individuals. Indeed, new research from the CDC supports this contention, stating, "Heroin use among nonmedical users of opioid pain relievers increased between 2002–2004 and 2008–2010, with most reporting nonmedical use of opioid pain relievers before initiating heroin" (Jones, 2013).

Figure 2.4 presents the main data series that underlie the CDU estimates. Past-month heroin users in NSDUH, heroin treatment admissions, and heroin overdose deaths all show increases starting in 2006 or 2007. It is unclear what caused the large spike in past-month heroin use reported in the 2006 NSDUH.[12]

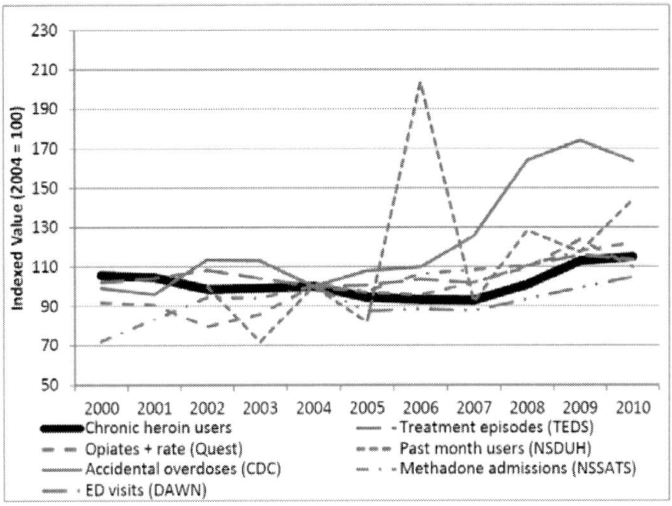

Figure 2.4. Comparison of Indexed National Heroin Use Series, 2000–2010 (100 = 2004 Value).

Table 2.4. Millions of Chronic Heroin Users by Frequency, 2000–2010

	2000	2001	2002	2003	2004	2005	2006	2007	2008	2009	2010
21+ days in past month	0.9	0.9	0.9	0.9	0.9	0.8	0.8	0.8	0.9	1.0	1.0
11–20 days in past month	0.2	0.2	0.2	0.2	0.2	0.2	0.2	0.2	0.2	0.2	0.2
4–10 days in past month	0.3	0.3	0.2	0.2	0.2	0.2	0.2	0.2	0.2	0.3	0.3

Note: Figure 2.3 displays the some of the uncertainty surrounding these CDU estimates. Since the distribution of CDUs is similar for ADAM-I (2000–2003) and ADAM-II (2007–2010), we average these figures and apply the same ratio to all years (69 percent, 14 percent, 17 percent). Thus, these three groups all display the same trends.

It is difficult to estimate the total number of heroin CDUs with great precision and even harder to break those totals down by type of CDU. Our analyses from ADAM suggest that about two-thirds of CDUs are in the 21-days-or-more group (Table 2.4); that is a considerably larger proportion than for cocaine.

2.3.3. Methamphetamine

Figure 2.5 presents estimates of the number of chronic meth users. Our middle estimates of the number of chronic meth users increased from 0.9 million in 2000 to 1.6 million in 2010. Similar to Figure 2.1, the error band in this figure is only driven by one source of uncertainty: the 95-percent confidence interval surrounding the predicted share of adult male arrest events involving a positive drug test for methamphetamine.

Results can only be as reliable as the underlying data, and we harbor serious reservations about the data available on methamphetamine. Other researchers have noted that national datasets do not do a good job of capturing meth consumption (Nicosia et al., 2009), and there are several reasons to be concerned for our particular analysis:

- ADAM almost exclusively covers urban counties and meth has been a serious problem in rural America.
- We do not have ADAM data for the 2004–2006 period when meth consumption apparently peaked.
- NSDUH changed how it asked about methamphetamine in the middle of the decade, making it difficult to compare data about meth prevalence and use days before and after 2007.
- We are not confident about using the QUEST data for methamphetamine (see Technical Report).
- We cannot separate methamphetamine deaths from other psychostimulants in the mortality data. When counties report drug arrests to the FBI, methamphetamine gets combined with "other dangerous drugs."

These issues dramatically increase the uncertainty concerning the model results, which is captured in the very large error bands.

While our CDU estimate for 2000 (875,000) is roughly similar to what was produced for the previous report (823,000) and both series display an increase through 2005, our model generates a much steeper increase. Figure 2.6 displays some of the series that underlie our CDU estimates as well as three other national series. Our CDU estimates closely follow the trend observed for meth treatment admissions as well as deaths involving psychostimulants, which includes meth.[13] The QUEST testing data that begin in 2002 show an increase in positive tests for methamphetamine through 2005.

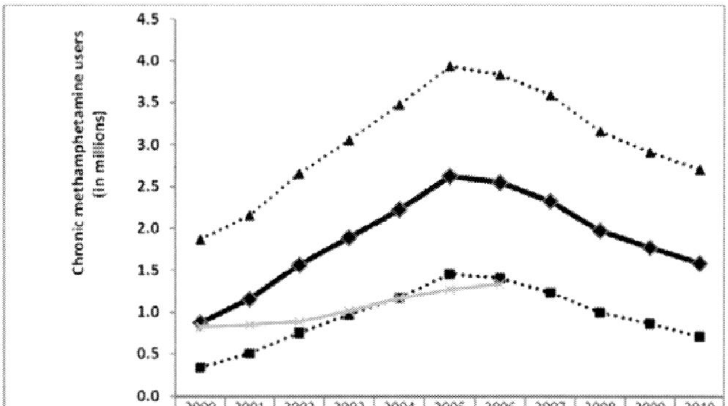

	2000	2001	2002	2003	2004	2005	2006	2007	2008	2009	2010
Middle	0.9	1.2	1.6	1.9	2.2	2.6	2.6	2.3	2.0	1.8	1.6
Lower	0.3	0.5	0.8	1.0	1.2	1.5	1.4	1.2	1.0	0.9	0.7
Higher	1.9	2.2	2.7	3.1	3.5	3.9	3.8	3.6	3.2	2.9	2.7
ONDCP (2012)	0.8	0.9	0.9	1.0	1.2	1.3	1.3				

Figure 2.5. Estimated Number of Chronic Methamphetamine Users, 2000–2010 (In Millions).

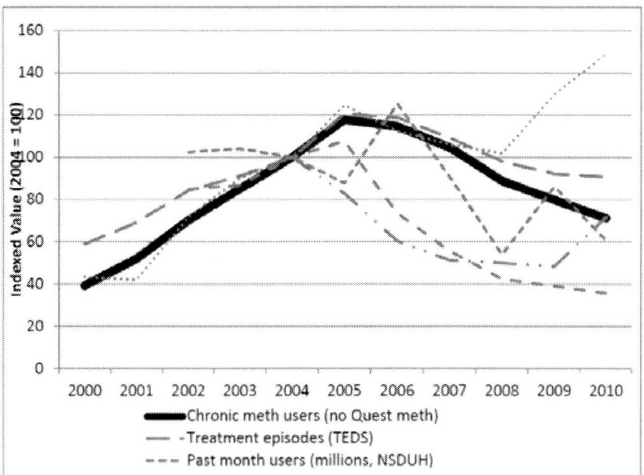

Figure 2.6. Comparison of Indexed National Methamphetamine Use Series, 2000–2010. (100 = 2004 Value).

Several factors show an increasing trend in meth consumption over the first half of the decade and a subsequent decline through 2008, but there is much less agreement after that year. We suggest that the most defensible position concerning trends in meth consumption from 2008 to 2010 is simply to acknowledge the data are insufficient to provide clear guidance.

Table 2.5 presents the composition of chronic meth users by intensity, with all three intensity groups containing about one-third of the CDU. There is no heavy concentration of daily/near-daily users, as is the case with heroin, nor is there a large group of daily/near-daily users widely separated from a large group of relatively infrequent users with few in between, as with cocaine.

Table 2.5. Millions of Chronic Methamphetamine Users by Frequency, 2000–2010

	2000	2001	2002	2003	2004	2005	2006	2007	2008	2009	2010
21+ days in past month	0.3	0.4	0.5	0.6	0.7	0.8	0.8	0.7	0.6	0.6	0.5
11–20 days in past month	0.3	0.3	0.5	0.6	0.7	0.8	0.7	0.7	0.6	0.5	0.5
4–10 days in past month	0.4	0.5	0.6	0.7	0.9	1.0	1.0	0.9	0.8	0.7	0.6

Note: Figure 2.5 displays the some of the uncertainty surrounding these CDU estimates. Since the distribution of CDUs is similar for ADAM-I (2000–2003) and ADAM-II (2007–2010), we average these figures and apply the same ratio to all years (36 percent, 30 percent, 34 percent). Thus, these three groups all display the same trends.

3. Expenditures on Cocaine, Heroin, and Methamphetamine

3.1. Introduction

This Section generates annual estimates of total spending on cocaine, heroin, and meth for 2000 through 2010. Similar to our estimates of CDUs and the previous version of this report (ONDCP, 2012c), our figures are rooted in ADAM. We present expenditure estimates by user types, highlighting that those who use 21 or more days in the past month account for the majority of spending.

Here, the focus is on the total amount of cash spent by the final purchaser of the drugs. We do not include the value of drugs for those who did not pay cash (e.g., those who got them for free, those who traded them for sex or a stolen good, those who produced their own—which only applies to meth). We do this for multiple reasons. First, we do not want to double-count expenditures. If someone buys an eight-ball of cocaine (3.5 grams) for $150 and trades away half of it, the amount spent on that cocaine is $150, not $150 plus the value of the good that was traded—that would be double counting. Second, knowing how much cash is spent and working its way through distribution channels is important for thinking about organized crime revenues and black markets. Third, placing a market value on stolen/traded good (e.g., value of sex) is difficult. While ADAM does ask respondents to place a value on bartered goods, it is unclear whether users are getting market value in return for the drugs.

3.2. Methodology

A detailed account of our approach and how it differs from the previous version of this study are included in the Technical Report. To estimate CDU expenditures, we first grouped ADAM adult male arrestees into four past-month drug-use categories: light (one to three days), medium (four to ten), heavy (11 to 20), and daily/near-daily (21 or more). We find that the prices and purchase patterns differ significantly across these use groups. This is not a necessary step analytically, but it helps to identify the sources of change over time with more detail than a method generating a single aggregate annual metric. We have explicitly modeled them independently before aggregating to a bottom-line chronic user expenditure estimate to highlight sources of variability and uncertainty.

There are six main steps to generating national expenditure estimates for each drug:

> Step 1. Generate arrestee-level monthly spending estimates by multiplying the value of the most recent purchase by the number of purchases that day and past-month purchase days reported.
>
> Step 2. Create average ADAM county–level monthly expenditure estimates for each past-month chronic-use category (four to ten, 11–20, and 21 or more days). For counties in ADAM-I, averages are based on available data from 2000–2003. For counties

in ADAM-II (10 of which are also in ADAM-I), averages are generated for the 2000–2003 period and the 2007–2010 period.

Step 3. Use the change between the periods 2000–2003 and 2007–2010 for ADAM-II counties to extrapolate the linear growth between these periods in the larger set of ADAM-I counties for which only 2000–2003 data are available.

Step 4. Extrapolate average annual expenditures for each past-month chronic-use category from the ADAM-I county estimates to the nation using UCR arrest data; creating an arrest-weighted national average expenditure estimate based on the number of arrestees reported in each UCR county, chronic-use category prevalence rates, and average expenditures estimated from ADAM. This assumes the distribution of users in each chronic-use category in the nation is similar to that seen in ADAM counties.

Step 5. Generate expenditure estimate for chronic users by multiplying the estimated number of users in each chronic-use category in each county-year by the average expenditure for that category.

Step 6. Estimate total annual national expenditures by multiplying total CDU annual expenditures by a drug-specific adjustment factor to account for spending by non-CDUs.

3.2.1. Steps 1-3: Estimating Average Monthly Spending by User Type

These steps are straightforward and only require data from ADAM-I (2000–2003) and ADAM-II (2007–2010). The first two steps require nothing more than cleaning the data and computing county-year averages. To account for the lack of ADAM data for 2004 to 2006, we use the change between the periods 2000–2003 and 2007–2010 for ADAM-II counties to extrapolate the linear growth between these periods in the larger set of ADAM-I counties for which only 2000–2003 data are available.

Tables 3.1–3.3 display average monthly spending for cocaine, heroin, and meth by user type as well as a weighted average. We adjust annual expenditure estimates for inflation using the Bureau of Labor Statistics' All-Urban Consumer Price Index, which increased by 27 percent from 2000 to 2010.

While the weighted averages for cocaine and heroin both start close to $1,000, they exhibit very different trends. In real terms, average spending on cocaine declined throughout the decade by 15 percent while average spending on heroin increased by roughly 33 percent. The decrease for cocaine is largely driven by a decrease in average spending for the 21-days- or-more group (in fact, this decrease is offset by an increase in spending for those in the four-to-ten-days group).

Average meth spending slightly increased through the decade, but the weighted average was considerably lower than it was for cocaine and heroin.

This is likely driven by the relatively even distribution of users across frequency groups for meth compared to the skewed results for heroin and bimodal distribution for cocaine (i.e., relatively few users in the 11–20 day group).

Table 3.1. Average Monthly Cocaine Expenditures (2010 dollars)

	21+ days in past month	11–20 days in past month	4–10 days in past month	Weighted Average
2000	2,171	965	356	1,035
2001	2,128	959	359	1,015
2002	2,085	953	361	997
2003	2,041	947	364	985
2004	1,998	941	367	977
2005	1,954	936	369	968
2006	1,911	930	372	955
2007	1,868	924	374	938
2008	1,824	918	377	919
2009	1,781	912	380	901
2010	1,737	906	382	883

Table 3.2. Average Monthly Heroin Expenditures (2010 dollars)

	21+ days in past month	11–20 days in past month	4–10 days in past month	Weighted Average
2000	1,486	342	206	1,089
2001	1,521	392	238	1,125
2002	1,556	442	270	1,161
2003	1,590	493	303	1,198
2004	1,625	543	335	1,234
2005	1,660	593	368	1,270
2006	1,695	644	400	1,306
2007	1,729	694	433	1,343
2008	1,764	744	465	1,381
2009	1,799	794	497	1,420
2010	1,834	845	530	1,457

Table 3.3. Average Monthly Methamphetamine Expenditures (2010 dollars)

	21+ days in past month	11–20 days in past month	4–10 days in past month	Weighted Average
2000	1,112	509	235	586
2001	1,126	521	228	599
2002	1,141	534	221	609
2003	1,155	546	214	617
2004	1,170	559	207	625
2005	1,184	572	200	632
2006	1,198	584	193	637
2007	1,213	597	186	642
2008	1,227	610	179	646
2009	1,241	622	172	651
2010	1,256	635	165	655

3.2.2. Steps 4-6: Estimating Average Monthly Spending by User Type

The next steps move from average CDU spending in ADAM counties to the rest of the country, including non-CDUs (i.e., those using one to three days in the previous month).

We use UCR adult male arrests to extrapolate our ADAM county estimates to represent county-level drug expenditures among arrestees nationally. We assume that the share of arrests reporting light, medium, heavy, and daily/near-daily use in ADAM is representative of the true mix of use among arrestees, and generate a single estimate of expenditures among arrestees for the ADAM counties with reliable UCR arrest data for adult males.

We generate a weighted average expenditure based on the number of arrests reported in each county; relatively more weight was given to expenditures in counties with more arrests and higher past-month prevalence rates. In constructing the weighted average, we consider only counties with UCR coverage above a certain threshold for each year from 2000 to 2010 to ensure that counties with erratic data were not given incorrect weights. National expenditures for each hard drug were estimated by multiplying the weighted average annual expenditure by the number of CDUs for each drug. To account for spending by non-CDUs, we multiply CDU expenditures by 1.12, 1.03, and 1.06 for cocaine, heroin, and meth, respectively. Please see the Technical Report for more information on the methodology.

3.3. Results

3.3.1. Cocaine

We estimate that cocaine expenditures are trending downward, driven mainly by decreasing chronic use (described in Section Two). We estimate cocaine expenditures fell by roughly 50 percent from $55 billion in 2000 to $28 billion in 2010. By comparison, the previous report estimated that cocaine expenditure remained roughly constant between $41 billion and $48 billion over 2000–2006 (see Figure 3.1). Both results (these and the prior report) show a stable estimate of cocaine expenditures from 2002–2006.

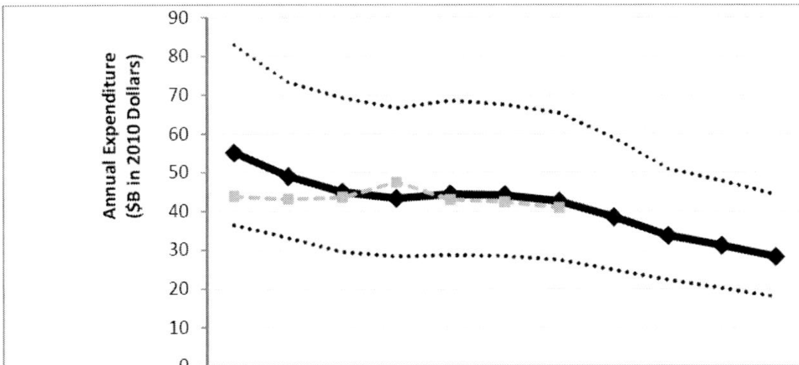

	2000	2001	2002	2003	2004	2005	2006	2007	2008	2009	2010
Middle	55.1	49.0	44.9	43.3	44.4	44.1	42.5	38.5	33.7	31.2	28.3
Lower	36.5	33.2	29.5	28.3	28.7	28.4	27.5	24.9	22.3	20.2	17.9
Higher	82.9	73.2	69.2	66.6	68.6	67.5	65.3	58.9	50.9	47.8	44.2
ONDCP (2012)	43.8	43.1	43.5	47.5	42.9	42.3	40.9				

Figure 3.1. Cocaine Expenditure Estimates2000–2010 (in billions of 2010 dollars).

Figure 3.2 reports cocaine expenditures by user type from 2000 to 2010. Reductions in spending among high-frequency cocaine users account for about 75 percent of the reduction in aggregate spending as the daily/near-daily user share of expenditures fell from about 54 percent to 47 percent between 2000 and 2010.

3.3.2. Heroin

We estimate annual expenditures for heroin that are approximately 50 percent higher than the previous report, while following a similar slow downward trend from $23 billion in 2000 to $21 billion in 2006. In the years that follow, heroin expenditures grow by more than 6 percent per year to $27 billion. Our estimates exceed the previous estimates due to our larger CDU size estimates. Figure 3.2 plots these differences.

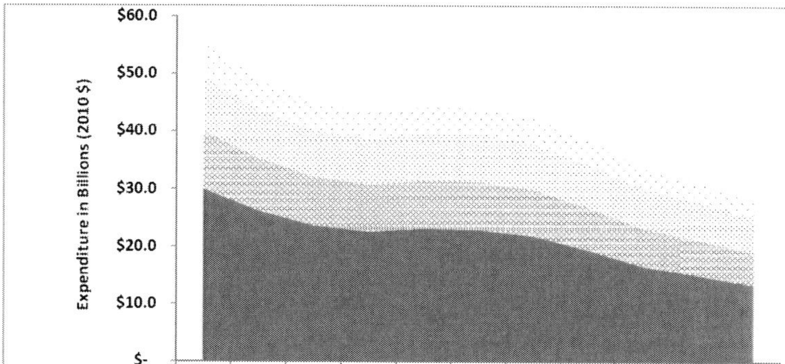

	2000	2001	2002	2003	2004	2005	2006	2007	2008	2009	2010
Light	$5.9	$5.2	$4.8	$4.6	$4.8	$4.7	$4.6	$4.1	$3.6	$3.3	$3.0
Weekly	$9.2	$8.5	$8.1	$7.9	$8.1	$8.2	$8.0	$7.5	$6.8	$6.5	$6.2
More than weekly	$10.1	$9.1	$8.4	$8.2	$8.4	$8.3	$8.1	$7.4	$6.6	$6.2	$5.7
Daily/Near-Daily	$30.0	$26.2	$23.6	$22.6	$23.1	$22.9	$21.9	$19.5	$16.7	$15.1	$13.4

Figure 3.2. Cocaine Expenditures by User Type, 2000–2010 (in billions of 2010 dollars).

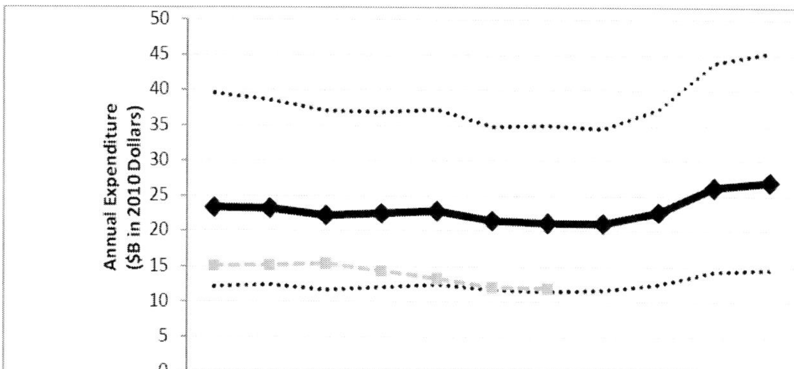

	2000	2001	2002	2003	2004	2005	2006	2007	2008	2009	2010
Middle	23.4	23.2	22.2	22.5	22.9	21.5	21.2	21.1	22.7	26.2	27.0
Lower	12.1	12.4	11.6	12.0	12.4	11.7	11.4	11.6	12.4	14.2	14.5
Higher	39.5	38.5	37.0	36.8	37.2	34.8	35.0	34.5	37.3	43.9	45.4
ONDCP (2012)	15.1	15.1	15.4	14.3	13.3	12.1	11.9				

Figure 3.3. Heroin Expenditure Estimates, 2000–2010 (in billions of 2010 dollars).

The vast majority of heroin expenditures come from daily/near-daily users (Figure 3.4)—though, as with cocaine, their contribution also fell between 2000 and 2010 from about 92 percent to 85 percent. Expenditures remained basically flat over the period until climbing between 2007 and 2010 (see Figure 3.3).

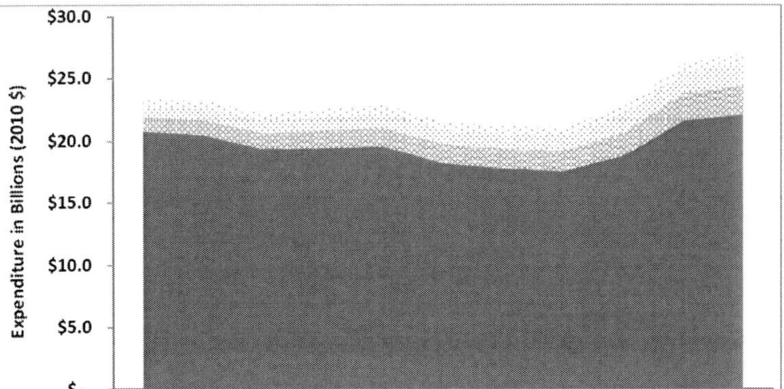

	2000	2001	2002	2003	2004	2005	2006	2007	2008	2009	2010
Light	$0.6	$0.6	$0.6	$0.6	$0.6	$0.6	$0.6	$0.6	$0.6	$0.7	$0.7
Weekly	$0.8	$0.9	$1.0	$1.1	$1.1	$1.2	$1.2	$1.3	$1.4	$1.7	$1.8
More than weekly	$1.1	$1.2	$1.3	$1.4	$1.5	$1.5	$1.6	$1.7	$1.9	$2.2	$2.4
Daily/Near-Daily	$20.8	$20.5	$19.4	$19.5	$19.6	$18.2	$17.8	$17.6	$18.8	$21.6	$22.1

Figure 3.4. Heroin Expenditures by User Type, 2000–2010 (in billions of 2010 dollars).

3.3.3. Methamphetamine

Our meth expenditure estimates generally show more volatility over time than the previous report. This is due in part to additional data used in our analysis. The trends in the previous version of the report for 2004 through 2006 are based largely on TEDS trends, which tend to be more stable than other drug market indicators. This may be because treatment facilities covered by TEDS face budget, capacity, or other limitations that do not exist for other proxies of illegal drug consumption.

It is feasible that metrics based on facilities at capacity will report relatively stable trends in drug-related treatment admissions despite excess demand for services.

Conversely, facilities under capacity may face funding reductions leading to reductions in all admissions, leaving a constant proportion of admissions for a particular substance.

Due to considerable uncertainty in chronic-user rates, only general patterns can be gleaned from these data (Figure 3.5). Of note, we estimate much faster growth of annual CDUs from similar year 2000 previously reported.

However, our annual per-CDU expenditures are approximately 45–55 percent below the previous estimate. When taken together, our estimates quickly surpass ONDCP (2012c) before peaking in 2005, perhaps driven by some combination of enforcement and treatment efforts such as the Combat Methamphetamine Epidemic Act of 2005 or substitution of legal prescription psychostimulant drugs.

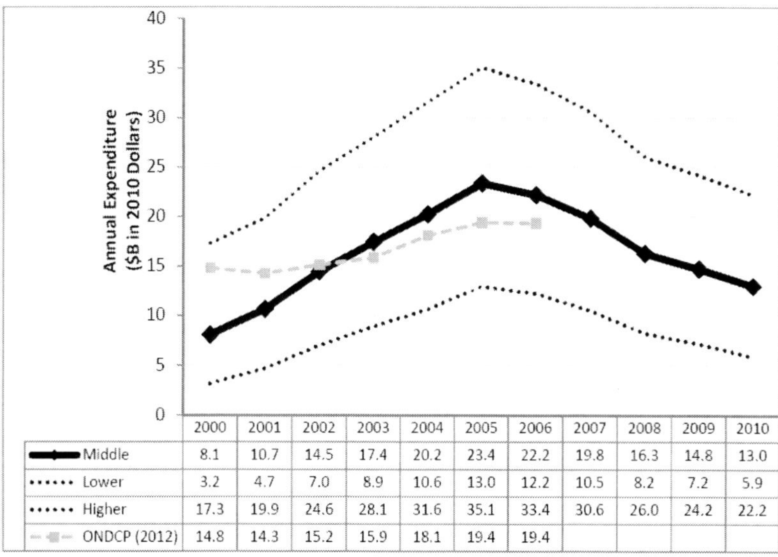

	2000	2001	2002	2003	2004	2005	2006	2007	2008	2009	2010
Middle	8.1	10.7	14.5	17.4	20.2	23.4	22.2	19.8	16.3	14.8	13.0
Lower	3.2	4.7	7.0	8.9	10.6	13.0	12.2	10.5	8.2	7.2	5.9
Higher	17.3	19.9	24.6	28.1	31.6	35.1	33.4	30.6	26.0	24.2	22.2
ONDCP (2012)	14.8	14.3	15.2	15.9	18.1	19.4	19.4				

Figure 3.5. Meth expenditures, 2000–2010 (in billions of 2010 dollars).

The daily/near-daily user share of methamphetamine use remained basically constant over time, at just over 60 percent, despite the rapid escalation and decline of expenditures (Figure 3.6).

A slight decrease in the contribution of weekly chronic users from about 16 percent to 12 percent is estimated, though this trend is unlikely to be statistically significant.

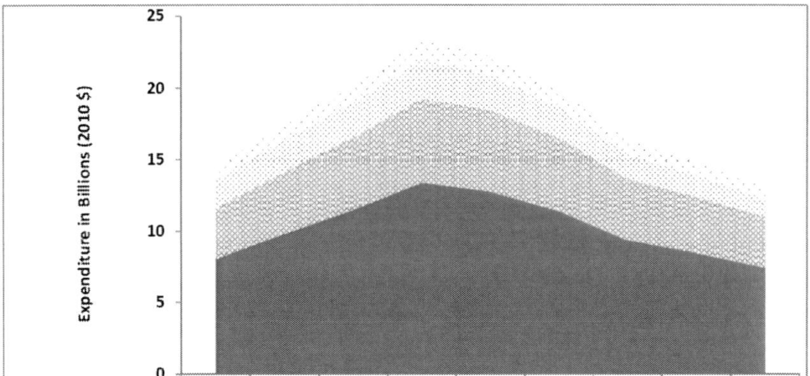

	2002	2003	2004	2005	2006	2007	2008	2009	2010
Light	$0.9	$1.1	$1.2	$1.4	$1.4	$1.2	$1.0	$0.9	$0.8
Weekly	$2.0	$2.2	$2.5	$2.7	$2.5	$2.1	$1.7	$1.5	$1.2
More than weekly	$3.6	$4.3	$5.0	$5.9	$5.7	$5.1	$4.3	$4.0	$3.6
Daily/Near-Daily	$8.0	$9.8	$11.5	$13.4	$12.8	$11.4	$9.3	$8.4	$7.4

Figure 3.6. Methamphetamine Expenditures by User Type, 2000–2010 (in billions of 2010 dollars).

4. ESTIMATING COCAINE, HEROIN, AND METHAMPHETAMINE CONSUMPTION

4.1. Introduction

The general approach for estimating the pure quantities for cocaine, heroin, and methamphetamine consumed is to divide national expenditure estimates for each substance by national average price paid per pure gram purchased, with a minor adjustment to account for in-kind (barter) transactions as opposed to cash purchases.

The national expenditure estimates for the numerator are presented in Section Three. The denominator is generated using purchase value information from ADAM and applying the RAND/Institute for Defense Analysis (IDA) method for generating purity-adjusted price information from STRIDE (Arkes, Pacula, Paddock, Caulkins, & Reuter, 2004; Fries et al., 2008). While our approach is generally similar to what was done in previous studies, there are some differences. Further, we are able to take advantage of additional years of data for our calculations.

4.2. Methodology

Details of our methodological approach are reported in the Technical Report. This Section provides an overview of how we calculated the numerators and denominators for our consumption estimates.

4.2.1. Generating the Numerator

Section Three estimated the amount of ***money*** spent buying drugs, but drug users sometimes barter goods (perhaps stolen) and services (e.g., serving as a lookout for a dealer) instead. If we merely divided monetary expenditures by price, we would obtain only the quantity purchased with cash, not the total quantity obtained. Similar to ONDCP (2001), we increase monetary expenditures by one-eighth (multiply by 1.125) to account for how much more users acquire and use than they buy with money.[14] In other words, we count drugs purchased by bartering goods and services but exclude home production. We are not aware of home production of heroin and cocaine in the United States, and people who reported obtaining marijuana most recently by growing it themselves in the 2010 NSDUH accounted for only about 3 percent of past-month days of use. However, it is not known what proportion of meth consumption is supplied by home-production, and that proportion may have varied over time with fluctuations in the availability of precursor chemicals.

The factor of 1.125 is more judgmental than data-driven. If a reader believed that barter-based acquisitions were more or less common than the 1.125 figure would suggest, we would not discourage them from inserting their own judgments and tracing through the implications. For example, if one-fifth of purchases were made with in-kind payments, then the factor would be 1.25, not 1.125, and quantity consumed would be 1.25 / 1.125 = 10 / 9 as large as what we report. About the only thing one could say for certain is that since bartering for drugs does occur, omitting the adjustment altogether would create a downward bias in our quantity estimates.

4.2.2. Generating the Denominator

The denominator (price paid per pure gram obtained) is based on the familiar ONDCP price estimation methodology (e.g., Fries et al., 2008), but estimates prices at a smaller referent quantity, closer to the typical quantity purchased by a heavy user, and then makes a further adjustment to pay attention in detail to the distribution of purchase sizes reported by ADAM respondents.

The price series is derived from enforcement data, specifically the DEA's STRIDE database. There is an ongoing debate in the literature about whether STRIDE can be used to produce useful price series. We believe it can be (Arkes et al., 2008), but there are well-informed people who disagree (Horowitz, 2001). We will not revisit the particulars of that debate here, but obviously if those critics are correct, then our estimates of quantities consumed are seriously compromised.[15] Furthermore, even if STRIDE can be used to monitor price trends (in the sense that the percentage changes in some STRIDE-based benchmark is a reasonable proxy for the corresponding percentage changes in actual market prices), it is another matter entirely to use STRIDE to figure out the average amount spent per pure gram obtained. Part of this is just the possibility that those generating price observations in STRIDE might systematically pay more or less than what typical market participants pay (e.g., they might pay more because law enforcement agents have less incentive to bargain for the best price).

The other issue, though, is quantity discounts or, equivalently, price mark-ups. Heavy users of expensive drugs are often impoverished and unable to maintain large inventories of either cash or drugs; thus, the median retail purchase size that arrestees report for cocaine powder, crack, heroin, and meth is only $20. Retail price trends for these substances are customarily monitored at the level of one (pure) gram, which is a much larger purchase. Since illegal drugs are subject to very considerable quantity discounts, gram-level prices are not a good reflection of the average amount heavy users spend per pure gram obtained. Thus, we generate a new price series with lower "referent quantities" that are closer to the quantity (in pure grams) typically purchased for each drug in a street-level sale. These new price series suggest users are paying more per pure gram obtained and so are consuming less per dollar spent than would have been presumed in the past.

After validating our purity–adjusted price estimates against Fries et al. (2008) and our previous report (Arkes et al. 2004), we establish new amounts that are closer to the quantity (in pure grams) typically purchased for each drug in a street-level sale, shown in Table 4.1.

Since retail prices are often reported for transactions of one pure gram, these levels might initially seem low. Yet, if anything, these levels are conservative. At the average prices over the 2000–2010 period, these correspond to purchases of about $50 for crack and powder cocaine and $90–$100 for heroin and meth.

Table 4.1. Pure Gram Price Evaluation Levels for Each Drug (in pure grams)

	Crack Cocaine	Powder Cocaine	Heroin	Methamphetamine
Evaluation level	0.25	0.25	0.1	0.25

Table 4.2 displays prices per pure gram for crack, powder cocaine, heroin, and methamphetamine, along with the quantity discount factor for each substance. This can be interpreted as a metric of exponential price decline as the quantity purchased increases. A value of 1 suggests per-unit prices do not vary with the amount being purchased. Smaller values mean that price declines rapidly as small quantities increase. As previous research has found, powder and crack cocaine prices track closely, though not perfectly, over time. We find that both decrease from 2000 to 2006 then increase quickly in real terms until 2010.

Table 4.2. Price per Pure Gram at Our Preferred Evaluation Levels (2010 dollars)

	Crack Cocaine @ 0.25 pure gram	Powder Cocaine @ 0.25 pure gram	Heroin @ 0.1 pure gram	D-meth & unknown isomer @ 0.25 pure gram
2000	238	210	947	421
2001	226	256	833	428
2002	202	187	876	369
2003	193	186	853	383
2004	169	165	884	347
2005	166	164	843	289
2006	162	164	846	399
2007	168	166	784	387
2008	212	190	779	433
2009	240	229	857	387
2010	246	218	995	328
Quantity Discount Factor	0.787	0.741	0.416	0.691

4.3. Results

4.3.1. Cocaine

Figure 4.1 displays that cocaine consumption was fairly stable from 2000–2006 but then fell very sharply thereafter. There appears to be a 50-percent reduction in pure cocaine consumption in less than a five-period; this is unprecedented. While the uncertainty bands around these estimates are large, there is no denying that there was a tremendous shift in the latter part of the decade.

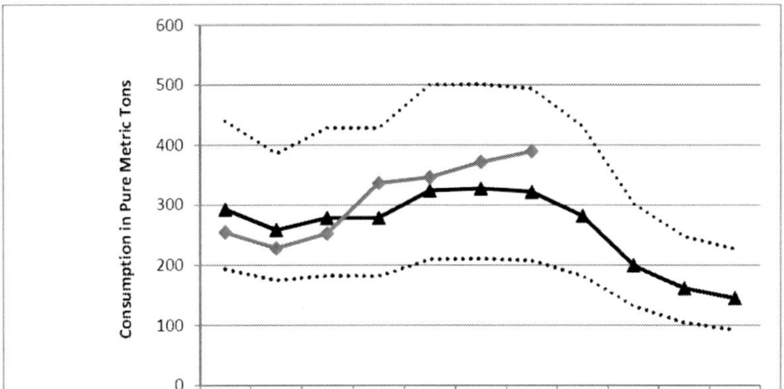

	2000	2001	2002	2003	2004	2005	2006	2007	2008	2009	2010
Middle	292	258	278	278	324	327	322	282	200	161	145
Lower	193	175	183	182	209	211	208	182	132	105	92
Higher	440	386	428	428	500	501	494	431	302	248	227
ONDCP (2012)	255	228	253	337	346	372	390				

Figure 4.1. Cocaine Consumption, 2000–2010 (pure MTs).

Our figures are very similar to those previously produced by ONDCP (2012c) for 2000–2002, but they diverge beginning in 2003. We show consumption remaining stable at 278 MTs for 2003, whereas the prior estimates report that consumption increased from 253 MTs in 2002 to 337 in 2003 — approximately a 33-percent increase. While the previous report suggested a 50-percent increase in pure cocaine consumption between 2000 and 2006, we calculate an increase closer to 10 percent. Even acknowledging that there are large uncertainties in both series, the difference in levels, especially for 2006, is striking (previous estimate = 390 MT; new estimate = 322 MT). To better understand what is driving this difference, Table 4.3 displays how these figures were generated. While our estimates of chronic cocaine users and the value of cocaine acquired are larger, their larger difference is with respect to average price paid per pure gram purchased.

Table 4.3. Comparing Cocaine Consumption Estimates for 2006

Calculated Estimates	ONDCP (2012)	Current Estimate
Chronic cocaine users (A)	2.77 million	3.21 million
Value of cocaine acquired (B)	$40.9 billion	$47.8 billion
$ per pure gram purchased (C)	$105	$149
Consumption = (B)/(C)	390 MTs	322 MTs

Notes: Figures from ONDCP (2012c) were reported in 2006 dollars ($97.12 and $37.8 billion) and converted to 2010 dollars using the Bureau of Labor Statistics' All-Urban Consumer Price Index. To generate the value of all cocaine acquired, we multiply our expenditure estimate presented in Section Three by 1.125.

4.3.2. Heroin

Figure 4.2 shows estimated heroin consumption has been fairly stable over time at approximately 25 MTs. These new estimates suggest consumption levels are below the estimates previously produced by ONDCP. Despite resting on fairly similar per-capita expenditure estimates and considerably higher CDU estimates, the consumption projections are lower because we now assess that heroin users are spending considerably more per pure unit purchased. That difference is due to our recognition that most use is by people who buy much less than one pure gram at a time.

4.3.3. Methamphetamine

Figure 4.3 shows that estimated meth consumption rose sharply to a peak in 2005 at roughly 85 MTs and then fell sharply through 2008. The series shows meth consumption as being stable from 2008 – 2010, but for reasons described in the Technical Report, we believe the evidentiary basis for this drug in those few years is particularly problematic. As was discussed in Section Two, the range depicted by the "higher" and "lower" estimates reflects only a portion of the uncertainty in these estimates, and may particularly understate the degree of uncertainty for meth in these years.

These new consumption estimates are 50–66 percent smaller in any given year than the previous analysis. While our CDU estimates are larger than previous projections, we estimate 50 percent less spending per chronic user in any given year (roughly $600 per month versus $1,200) and considerably higher prices per pure gram ($300–450 per pure gram versus $130–270, in

2010 dollars), again due at least in part to the previous reports basing prices per unit on purchases considerably larger than what arrestees report.

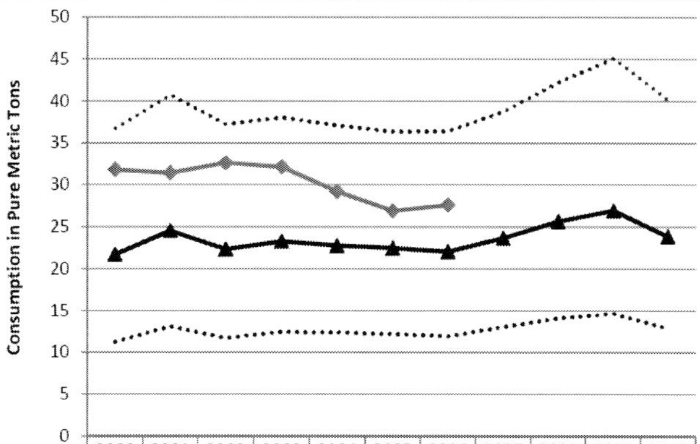

	2000	2001	2002	2003	2004	2005	2006	2007	2008	2009	2010
Middle	22	25	22	23	23	22	22	24	26	27	24
Lower	11	13	12	12	12	12	12	13	14	15	13
Higher	37	41	37	38	37	36	36	39	42	45	40
ONDCP (2012)	32	31	33	32	29	27	28				

Figure 4.2. Heroin Consumption, 2000–2010 (pure MTs).

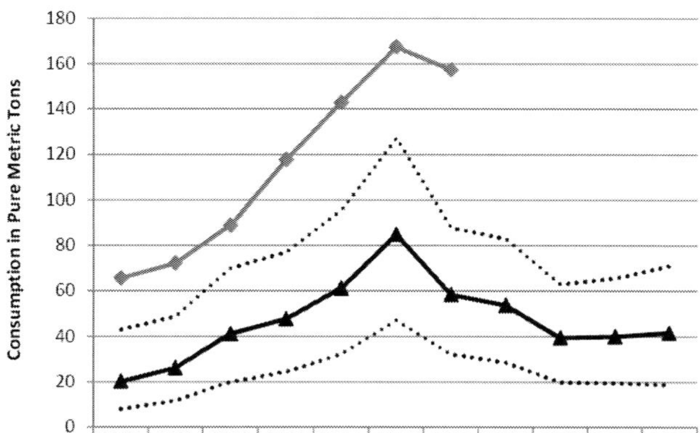

	2000	2001	2002	2003	2004	2005	2006	2007	2008	2009	2010
Middle	20	26	41	48	61	85	58	54	39	40	42
Lower	8	11	20	24	32	47	32	28	20	19	19
Higher	43	49	70	77	95	127	88	83	63	66	71
ONDCP (2012)	66	72	89	118	143	167	157				

Figure 4.3. Methamphetamine Consumption (pure MTs).

Domestically produced meth that is purchased—via cash or barter—is included in these consumption estimates; however, we include neither meth that is produced and consumed by the same individual, nor meth produced and gifted with no purchase. ADAM data suggest that few meth-using arrestees produce what they consume, but ADAM largely covers urban counties and meth production is believed to be more common in rural areas.

5. Marijuana

5.1. Introduction

The challenges in estimating market-related quantities for marijuana are quite different than those associated with estimating the same quantities for cocaine, heroin, and methamphetamine. As such, the approach taken is different than that employed for the other drugs. In particular, the marijuana user estimates are based primarily on NSDUH data, with some adjustments that tap information gleaned from ADAM and other sources. The consumption estimates combine NSDUH data on the number of user days with estimates of how much marijuana users consume on each day they use. The expenditure estimates are then derived from the consumption estimates using a marijuana price series derived from NSDUH (but corroborated by other sources) as well as information on potency.

This Section describes the main methods and discusses results about marijuana users, consumption, and expenditures. Additional information about the data sources and analyses is available in the Technical Report. The Section concludes by comparing our results with those previously reported by ONDCP (2012c).

5.2. Methodology

As with the other drugs, we focus on four categories of users, including occasional users (those who report using in the past month, but less than four days) and three levels of chronic users: weekly (four to ten days per month), more than weekly (11–20 days per month), and daily/near-daily (21 or more days per month). We also document the number of less frequent users, namely those who report past-year but not past-month use. Since general population surveys tend to undercount users, we apply some adjustments to these figures.

To estimate expenditures, we start with a metric that both NSDUH and ADAM ask about for an entire period, not just with respect to the most recent instance; that metric is days of use in the last month or year. Multiplying by quantity consumed per day of use converts that to quantity consumed in the last month or year. Multiplying again by price produces an estimate of spending.

Since the direct evidence concerning weight consumed per day comes from a particular era (2001– 2003) and marijuana potency has been increasing over the last decade, it is possible that grams consumed per day may have changed over time. Hence, we provide two expenditure series: a "constant grams" series, which assumes that the amount of marijuana consumed in a use day did not change over the decade (meaning that average THC consumption per use day increased); and a "constant THC" series, which assumes that THC consumption per use day did not change (meaning that the average marijuana consumption per use day decreased).

5.2.1. Marijuana Users

The number of marijuana users is estimated in two ways: first from NSDUH alone and then also by adjusting the NSDUH estimates with MTF and ADAM data to account for differential underreporting among youth and individuals involved in the criminal justice system.

5.2.1.1. Prevalence Estimates from NSDUH

We preserve the definitions of occasional and chronic users employed in prior versions of this report, but also report for three distinct subsets of chronic users: a) Daily/Near-Daily: those using 21 or more days in previous month; b) More than Weekly: 11–20 days in previous month; and c) Weekly: four to ten days in the previous month. Those using less than four days in the previous month align with the previous definition of occasional users. Light users are those using one to four times days in the previous month and Infrequent users are those using in the past year but not the past month. The number of past-month users has increased by roughly 20 percent from 2004 to 2010, and most of that increase is among the heaviest users (Table 5.1).

The counts of marijuana users (and, later, marijuana use days) include not only those who indicate directly that they have used marijuana, but also a modest number who deny using "marijuana" when asked about it in the standard battery of questions but who nonetheless do indicate later in the survey that they have used blunts, a particular form of marijuana use.[16] The impact of including them on the number of users is small; the impact on the number of use days is somewhat more significant, and therefore important to the calculation of quantity consumed.

Table 5.1. Number of Marijuana Users, by Intensity of Use (NSDUH)

Year	Infrequent	Light[a]	Weekly	More than Weekly	Daily/Near-Daily	Total, Past-Month Users
2000[b]	7,897,404	3,728,863	2,553,657	1,884,062	2,547,100	10,713,682
2001[b]	8,943,216	4,213,017	2,742,171	2,066,520	3,100,307	12,122,015
2002	11,352,301	4,620,674	3,562,462	2,582,778	3,817,922	14,583,836
2003	10,815,568	4,951,453	3,297,084	2,615,522	3,911,252	14,775,311
2004	10,917,262	5,125,332	3,107,401	2,584,386	4,164,693	14,981,812
2005	10,836,514	4,774,757	3,604,589	2,331,878	4,226,933	14,938,157
2006	10,439,821	4,851,109	3,307,378	2,943,745	4,203,008	15,305,240
2007	10,728,393	4,818,181	3,343,616	2,161,160	4,398,995	14,721,952
2008	10,357,957	5,062,140	2,986,563	2,768,616	4,782,539	15,599,858
2009	11,893,362	5,192,632	3,898,926	2,823,576	5,276,072	17,191,206
2010	11,746,901	5,111,656	4,068,273	2,858,795	5,961,035	17,999,759

[a] This category was referred to as "occasional users" in previous editions of this report.

[b] The 2000–2003 marijuana estimates are not perfectly comparable to the later years because of changes in survey questions and methods.

Thus, there are two discontinuities in the NSDUH data over time that should be noted. First, the questions about blunt use were added in 2004. Since inclusion of the blunt questions increases the number of respondents who admit to some form of marijuana use, this suggests that the figures from 2000–2003 may underestimate marijuana use. The more important (and well-documented) discontinuity results from the change in recruiting and sampling procedures that was implemented in 2002, when the National Household Survey on Drug Abuse (NHSDA) became NSDUH. This change increased reported users for marijuana and other drugs, making direct comparisons before and after 2002 difficult.

5.2.1.2. Addressing Misreporting in NSDUH

As other researchers have noted, while NSDUH likely captures a larger fraction of marijuana use than it does use of other illicit drugs, it most likely misses some users and usage nonetheless. When surveying respondents about sensitive behaviors, underreporting is a perennial concern. It is common to adjust marijuana consumption estimates upward. As noted above, the authors of earlier editions of this report used an adjustment of 1.33. Others have used somewhat smaller (e.g., Kilmer, Caulkins, Pacula, & Reuter, 2011) or even larger adjustments (e.g., Gettman, 2007).

Three distinct phenomena can contribute to a downward bias: The NSDUH sample does not include homeless not in shelters, active-duty military, and institutionalized populations like the incarcerated (some categories of which may contain a disproportionate number of drug users); heavy users may be more likely to be missed even if they are in the NSDUH sampling frame, rendering SAMHSA's adjustments for nonresponse insufficient; and individuals may not be truthful about their drug use behaviors—both whether and how much they use. Harrison, Martin, Enev, and Harrington (2007) focused only on whether individuals are truthful about whether they use. All three phenomena should be considered, but the available evidence allows quantification of only some of them. On the other hand, we do go beyond past estimates by disaggregating the NSDUH data into subcategories that facilitate examination of the extent to which the NSDUH user estimates are biased downward, and apply separate adjustments to each category. Details are provided in Section 6.2 of the Technical Report. In particular, we adjust the prevalence rates of youth users to match the (age-specific) prevalence rates reported by MTF, and we adjust the prevalence rates of NSDUH users who report past-year involvement in the criminal justice system to match those reported in ADAM. The NSDUH adults not involved in criminal justice are adjusted upward by a factor of 1.25, based on Kilmer et al. (forthcoming and 2011).[17]

Figure 5.1 compares the unadjusted NSDUH figures and the population-adjusted estimates. The population-adjusted total number of past-month users in 2010 is about 25 million, as opposed to 18 million without the adjustment. The method employed here yields annual estimates close to the ONDCP estimates this document revises, as the prior figures all fall between our adjusted and unadjusted estimates. For example, we estimate 20.7 users in 2006 (adjusted), a slight upward revision to the previous ONDCP estimate of 19.2 million (see Figure 5.10 for a comparison).

5.2.2. Marijuana Consumption

Marijuana consumption is estimated from NSDUH-based data on the number of past-month use days, combined with information on how much marijuana users consume on each day that they use. The NSDUH-based estimate is adjusted in either of two ways: it is scaled up by the ratio of the population-adjusted estimate of users to the NSDUH-only estimate of users; and it is scaled up by a factor reflecting an estimate of the gap between survey-generated and supply-generated measures of alcohol consumption in the United States. The latter adjustment is substantially greater than the former; they yield two distinct estimates.

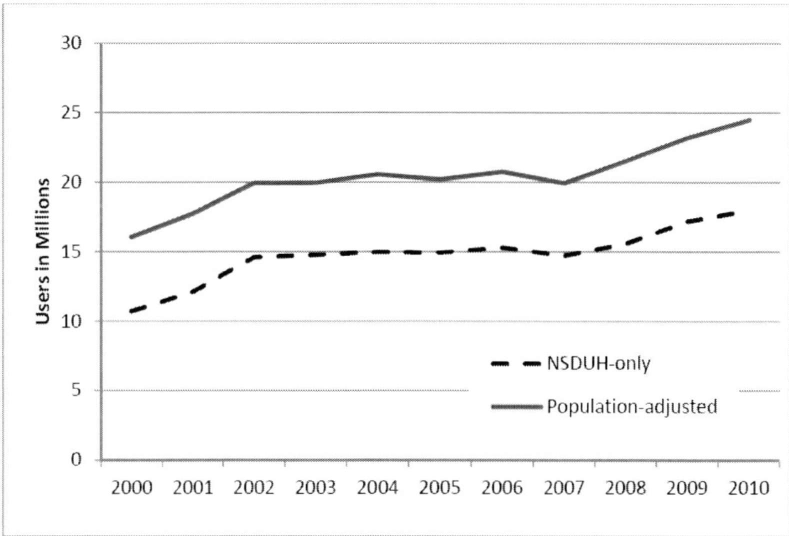

Note: The 2000-2003 marijuana estimates are not perfectly comparable to the later years because of changes in survey questions and methods.

Figure 5.1. Two Estimates of Marijuana Past-30-Day Users.

5.2.2.1. NSDUH Past-Month Use Days

Past-month use days are calculated for all the intensity-of-use groups—light, weekly, more than weekly, and daily/near-daily. Multiplying by 12 generates the annual number of use days for each group. These are illustrated in Figure 5.2. Note the rather dramatic increase in use days in recent years, concentrated among the heaviest users and accounted for largely by the increase in the number of users.

5.2.2.2. Amount of Marijuana Consumed per Day

It is a challenge to estimate daily marijuana consumption for a single point in time, let alone how it has varied over a decade. We have some information about grams consumed per day circa 2002 based on joints per day by user group from NESARC and on grams per joint based on RAND's previous analysis of ADAM 2000–2003 (Kilmer, Caulkins, MacCoun, Pacula, & Reuter, 2010b). This provides us a baseline estimate of the number of grams of marijuana consumed per use day (assuming that those who consumed marijuana other than by smoking joints reported an amount that was equivalent to what they usually consumed during a use day). This analysis suggests that at that time the number of joints/day was 1.68 for light users, 1.92 for weekly and more than weekly users, and 3.87 for daily/near-daily users. Based on a variety of considerations, the amount of marijuana in a typical joint is assumed to be 0.43 grams/joint. See Section 6.3 of the Technical Report for additional information on the data and calculations.

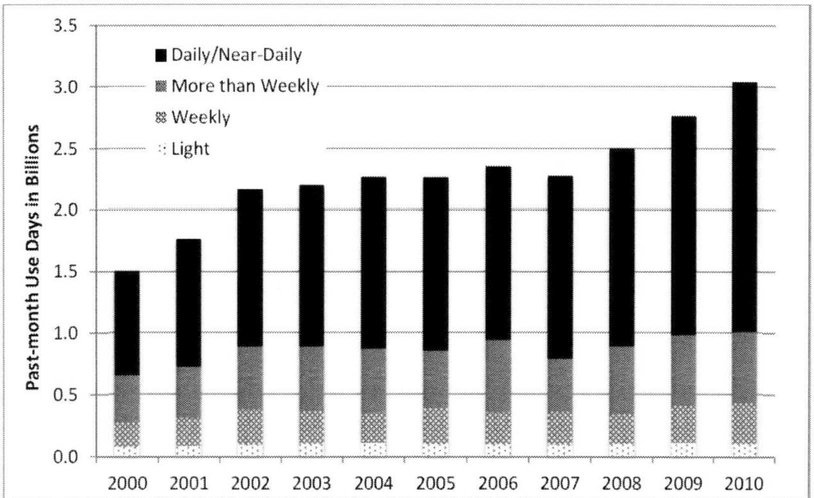

Note: The 2000–2003 marijuana estimates are not perfectly comparable to the later years because of changes in survey questions and methods.

Figure 5.2. Total Annual Marijuana Use Days (NSDUH, billions of use days).

5.3.2.3. Modes of Consumption and Sharing

The issue of sharing has important implications for how to interpret consumption estimates, which are based on multiplying the number of joints by grams per joint. Specifically, these figures could be overestimates if, for example, two individuals sharing one joint both reported that they consumed one joint. This is a real possibility with the NESARC data since there is no choice less than one.

Marijuana is being used in an increasing array of forms, not just in traditional joints. An alternative form of particular importance and for which NSDUH provides some data is "blunts." Many believe blunts include more marijuana that is typically inserted in a regular joint or pipe. There is very little empirical evidence on this, but a study with marijuana treatment seekers that asked them to roll blunts and joints with oregano suggests that blunts may be roughly 50 percent larger (Mariani, Brooks, Haney, & Levin, 2011):

> These data call into question the assumptions made in the Global Appraisal of Individual Needs (GAIN) (Dennis & Feeny, 2006), which suggests that one blunt is equivalent to two to six joints. The results of this study suggest that in treatment-seeking marijuana users the correct ratio is closer to 1.5 joints per blunt.

While this might seem to justify increasing grams per use day, we do not know if blunt users are more or less likely to share than those who consume via other modes. It could be that blunts contain more marijuana, but they are more likely to be shared. Another issue is that the survey questions do not clarify whether those who consumed via blunts on a use day only consumed blunts.

5.2.2.4. The Household Survey-Supply Consumption Gap

Alcohol researchers have noted that survey-based estimates of consumption often fall well below what is known to be consumed based on tax receipts or other supply side evidence. That is, underreporting of quantities consumed could be more severe than is underreporting of prevalence. This leads to the concern that the adjustments for survey underreporting described above may be inadequate. While it is extremely difficult to generate convincing estimates of marijuana supply given the illicit nature of the market (see Section Seven), it is relatively easy to generate supply measures in the case of alcohol, since alcohol is a legal substance that generates tax revenue and other sales-related data (Cook, 2008; Nelson et al., 2010). Cook uses NESARC and alcohol sales data from NIAAA to argue that NESARC "provides an estimate of per capita consumption that is about half of recorded per capita sales." This is consistent with an international review that found general population surveys underestimate alcohol consumption, sometimes by more than 50 percent (Gmel & Rehm, 2004). These studies suggest that it may be appropriate to inflate the NSDUH-only consumption estimates by a factor of two. Hence, our high estimate is determined by doubling the NSDUH-only estimate.

5.2.3. Marijuana Expenditures

Deriving spending estimates by multiplying use days by weight per day and price per unit weight is not the most direct approach. The household survey currently does ask respondents how much they spent on their ***most recent*** purchase. One could estimate spending over a period by multiplying that figure by the number of purchases made, but that would make a strong and as-yet untested assumption that the most recent purchase is a typical or representative purchase when it may not be. For one, if someone makes purchases of different sizes, some smaller (e.g., one gram) and some larger (e.g., one half-ounce) but consumes at a steady rate, then larger purchases may be followed by longer intervals beween purchases. Since the survey may be disproportionately likely to fall into such a time gap following a larger purchase, that could inflate spending estimates—possibly to a large degree. (See Section 6.1 of the Technical Report for a more detailed explanation of this problem.)

Marijuana expenditure estimates are generated by multiplying the consumption estimates described above by marijuana prices. Recall that we have three different estimates of consumption: a low one based on NSDUH measures of usage by past-month users; a middle estimate that is inflated to account for underreporting by specific populations; and a high one generated by multiplying the NSDUH-only estimated consumption by an estimated alcohol survey consumption gap. Since marijuana potency increased significantly between 2000 and 2010, we consider two scenarios for how users respond to changes in marijuana potency. The first assumes that users consume a constant number of grams of marijuana per day, so greater potency translates into greater THC consumption; the second assumes that users consume a constant amount of THC per day, so greater potency translates into smaller quantities being consumed per day.

5.2.3.1. Price per Gram of Marijuana

NSDUH data are our primary source of information on marijuana prices, but we also construct similar series using ADAM data to consider possible differences in prices paid by the populations captured by those two surveys. See Section 6.4 of the Technical Report for details. The price series used for the expenditure calculations is derived from small (i.e., less than or equal to 1 oz.) purchases in NSDUH; it varies from $7.14 in 2000 up to $7.50 in 2004 and back down to $7.11 in 2010 (in 2010 dollars).

It is common to base price series on STRIDE data. Fries et al. (2008) provide marijuana price series based on STRIDE, and we use STRIDE data for the other drugs, so it is worth mentioning why we do not base the marijuana prices on STRIDE. For one, STRIDE is a convenience sample based on law enforcement operations; it is not in any way a representative, let alone a random, sample of market participants. This fundamental limitation is sometimes overlooked for cocaine/crack, heroin, and meth because there are few (if any) alternatives. Further, the marijuana data in STRIDE are concentrated in a few cities that are not necessarily representative of the very different markets for marijuana that exist across the United States due to a variety of factors including: proximity to Mexican and Canadian borders, access to medical marijuana dispensaries, and differences in marijuana enforcement priorities. Finally, marijuana observations in STRIDE are not chemically analyzed to determine potency the way that purity is reported for the other drugs, so STRIDE does not offer more information on marijuana quality than do NSDUH or ADAM.

5.2.3.2. Trends in Marijuana Potency

Over the last 20 years, it has become standard practice to work with purity-adjusted prices for cocaine, heroin, and methamphetamine, not just the "raw" price per gram, unadjusted for purity. Marijuana is more complicated, because it contains many different psychoactive chemicals, but THC is the most important, so there is likewise an argument for working with marijuana prices adjusted for THC potency. That has not been standard practice in the past, but we do attempt to factor potency trends into our estimates here. This is clearly a topic worthy of additional methodological research.

The basic concern is that since potency has been trending upward, this might have changed the average amount or weight consumed per day of use. The argument for consuming fewer grams is straightforward. Potency affects the amount consumed per unit of intoxication. Roughly speaking, one-third of a gram of sinsemilla containing 15-percent THC can provide as much intoxication as one gram of commercial-grade marijuana that contains 5-percent THC. So when potency goes up, the weight of marijuana consumed per day of use ***may*** go down if users adjust consumption to keep the amount of THC per day of use stable.

On the other hand, even though more potent variants are more expensive per unit weight, the overall trend in potencies relative to prices is that the price per unit of THC has been falling, after adjusting for inflation. Since lower prices trigger greater consumption for all sorts of goods, that might mean THC consumption per day of use has risen. Indeed, since real prices have been falling, if the conditional price elasticity of THC consumption with respect to

THC prices were large enough, then in theory that could even lead to greater weights being consumed per day of use, although we would guess that probably has not happened. At any rate, failing to adjust for potency trends might bias estimates of marijuana spending.

To complicate matters, there is not just one type of marijuana. There are various strains, and there are attributes of marijuana besides THC content that affect its price, including presence of other cannabinoids and subjective notions of appearance. Broadly speaking, it appears that there has been both increasing potency within type and also a change in composition so that higher potency types now account for a larger share of the market, with the market composition effect perhaps being the more important.

As a first step toward trying to reflect marijuana quality in this analysis, we distinguish between two types of marijuana: higher-potency "sinsemilla" and lower-potency "commercial grade." There is no single data source that tracks how much sinsemilla is being consumed in the United States over time. The national drug use surveys (e.g., NSDUH, MTF) do not ask respondents about the type or potency of marijuana—and even if they did, it is not clear that users could or would provide reliable information. Thus, researchers are forced to combine insights from multiple sources to approximate levels and trends.

A number of indicators support the idea that the sinsemilla share of marijuana consumed in the United States increased from 2000 to 2010; however, neither the magnitude of the increase nor the current levels are known. Based on our analyses of market transactions from NSDUH and other sources, we assume that sinsemilla's "market share" increased from 10 percent in 2000 to 20 percent in 2010. (We use round figures to avoid suggesting that these figures are precise.)

Furthermore, average THC levels have also increased within each type. The increase in average potency for sinsemilla is modest; sinsemilla was already highly potent in 2000. The more important change seems to be for the commercial-grade marijuana, which still accounts for a sizable share of the market: Average THC for kilobrick seizures increased by more than one-third over the decade. Since commercial-grade prices seem to be fairly stable over the decade (possibly even decreasing after adjusting for inflation), consumers now pay less to achieve the same level of intoxication. Overall we estimate that the weighted average of marijuana potency has increased from 5.2 percent THC in 2000 to 8.1 percent THC in 2010. Details are provided in the Technical Report. As noted, the implications of these figures for total marijuana consumption and spending depend on one's beliefs about whether

THC consumption per typical use day increased over the decade or remained constant. If weight consumed per day stayed constant, then THC consumed per day would have increased; if THC consumed per day stayed constant, then weight consumed per day would have fallen – necessitating an adjustment to get spending estimates correct. This issue of different types of marijuana could become even more important in the future, if the recent trend toward proliferation of alternative forms of use continues (vaporizer pens, butane hash oil, "dabbing", etc.).

5.3. Results

This section discusses the marijuana results, first concentrating on prevalence, then moving on to consumption and finally to expenditures. The section that follows compares these results to the previous version of ***What America's Users Spend on Illicit Drugs*** (ONDCP, 2012c).

5.3.1. Marijuana User Estimates and Adjusted Marijuana User Estimates

Figure 5.3 plots the number of marijuana users in each of the five categories of usage intensity, derived directly from NSDUH and its predecessor NHSDA. Leaving aside the two pre-NSDUH years, the trends are largely flat or slightly increasing, with the notable exception of large increases in the number of the heaviest (i.e., daily/near-daily) users. Indeed, the daily/near-daily users now constitute the largest category of past-month users.[18] The population-adjusted estimate, with the breakdown of users by intensity, is depicted in Figure 5.4. The increase in the last few years of the decade is largely associated with an increase in the heaviest users, but the heaviest users still only account for just over a quarter of all past-month users.

5.3.2. Marijuana Consumption Estimates and Adjusted Marijuana Consumption Estimates

Figure 5.5 presents the three estimates of consumption: the lower estimate, calculated on the basis of NSDUH-generated use days; the middle one, which adjusts the first estimate in parallel to the population-adjusted number of users explained above in Section 5.1; and the higher estimate, which simply multiplies the NSDUH-only numbers by a factor of two, inspired by the alcohol survey consumption gap. By any of these measures, consumption was flat from 2002 to 2007, likely somewhere between 3,000 and 6,000 MTs. However, consumption appears to have increased substantially during the last few years of the decade, rising to somewhere between 4,000 and 8,500 MTs in 2010.

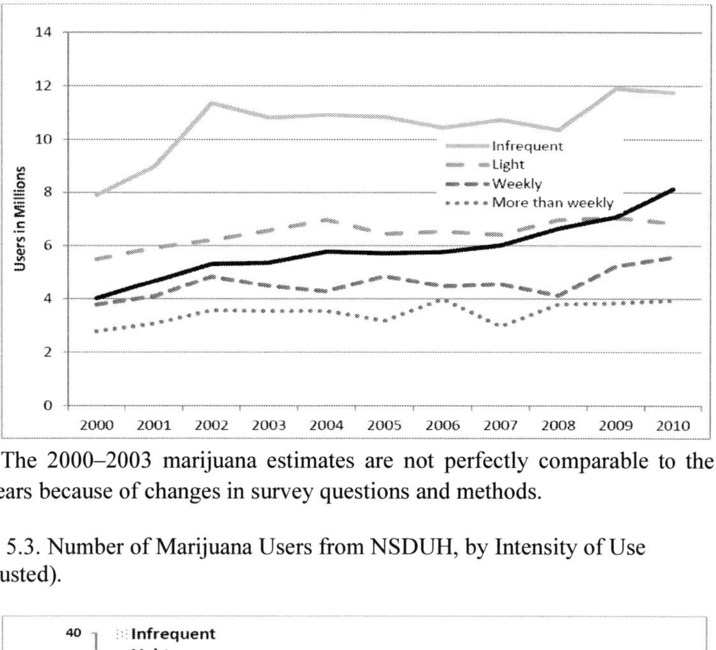

Note: The 2000–2003 marijuana estimates are not perfectly comparable to the later years because of changes in survey questions and methods.

Figure 5.3. Number of Marijuana Users from NSDUH, by Intensity of Use (unadjusted).

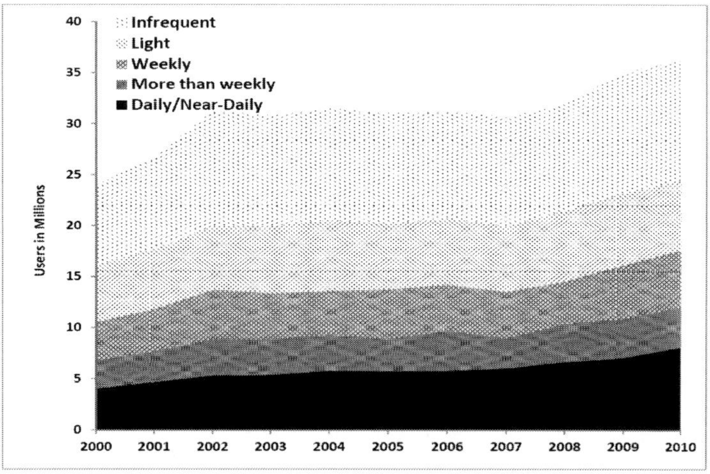

Note: The 2000–2003 marijuana estimates are not perfectly comparable to the later years because of changes in survey questions and methods.

Figure 5.4. Population-Adjusted Estimates of Marijuana Users by User Category.

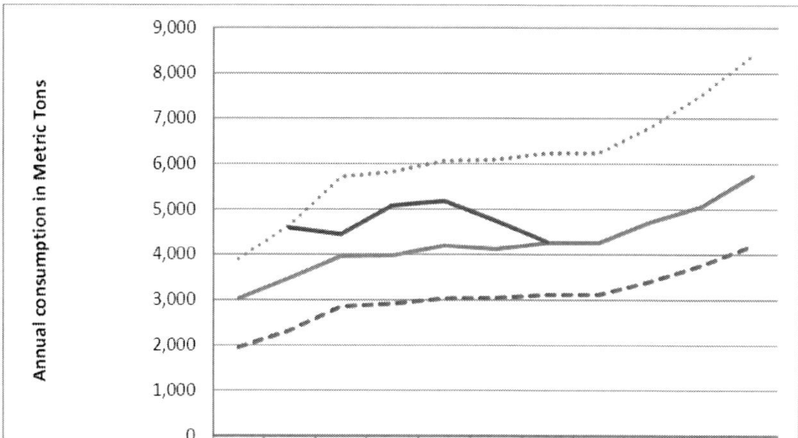

	2000	2001	2002	2003	2004	2005	2006	2007	2008	2009	2010
Middle	3,024	3,479	3,959	3,979	4,198	4,123	4,265	4,264	4,716	5,060	5,734
Lower	1,950	2,323	2,855	2,911	3,034	3,046	3,120	3,120	3,403	3,762	4,198
Higher	3,900	4,645	5,711	5,822	6,069	6,092	6,241	6,240	6,806	7,525	8,396
ONDCP (2012)		4,595	4,453	5,082	5,182	4,750	4,285				

Note: The 2000–2003 marijuana estimates are not perfectly comparable to the later years because of changes in survey questions and methods.

Figure 5.5. Estimates of Marijuana Consumption (MTs), 2000-2010.

5.3.3. Marijuana Expenditure Estimates, Ignoring Potency Trends

Combining the consumption estimates and the "NSDUH $\leq$ 1 oz" marijuana price series (see Section 6 of the Technical Report) generates the first set of expenditure estimates in Figure 5.6. Expenditures on marijuana in the United States were flat from 2002 to 2007, somewhere between $20 billion and $45 bilion, before increasing during the last few years of the decade, rising to somewhere between $30 billion and $60 billion in 2010. This set of results assumes users do not reduce their consumption in response to the increase in marijuana potency; the alternative is presented in Figure 5.9.

The corresponding breakdown of marijuana expenditures by user category is depicted in Figure 5.7.

The vast majority of the expenditures are by the heaviest—that is, daily/near-daily—users, even though they do not constitute the majority of the users.

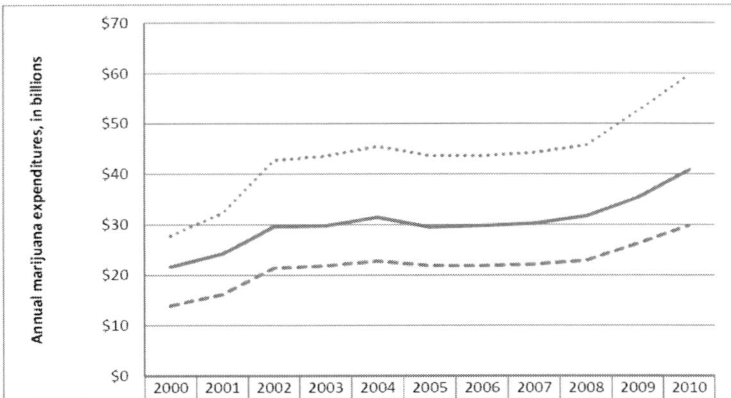

	2000	2001	2002	2003	2004	2005	2006	2007	2008	2009	2010
Middle	$21.6	$24.2	$29.6	$29.8	$31.5	$29.5	$29.8	$30.2	$31.7	$35.4	$40.8
Lower	$13.9	$16.1	$21.3	$21.8	$22.7	$21.8	$21.8	$22.1	$22.9	$26.3	$29.9
Higher	$27.8	$32.3	$42.7	$43.6	$45.5	$43.6	$43.6	$44.2	$45.7	$52.6	$59.7

Note: The 2000–2003 marijuana estimates are not perfectly comparable to the later years because of changes in survey questions and methods.

Figure 5.6. Estimates of Marijuana Expenditures, 2000–2010 (in billions of 2010 dollars).

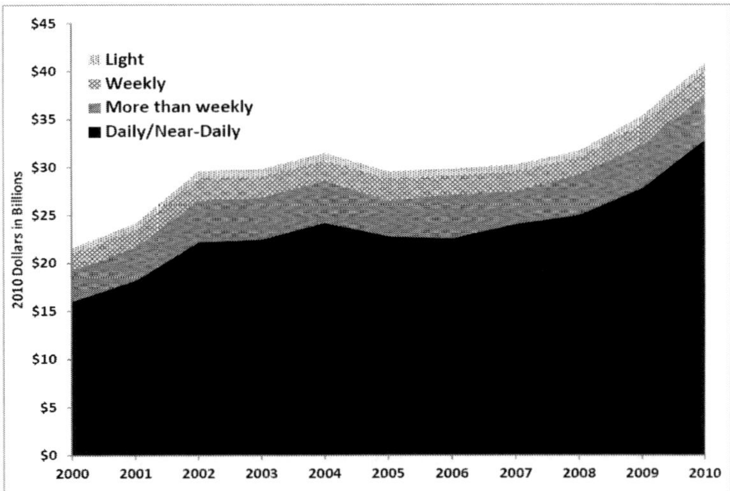

Note: The 2000–2003 marijuana estimates are not perfectly comparable to the later years because of changes in survey questions and methods.

Figure 5.7. Middle Estimate of Marijuana Expenditures by User Category (in billions of 2010 dollars).

5.3.4. Marijuana Expenditure Estimates, Accounting for Potency Trends

Given the increase in THC potency over time, we introduce a second expenditure series: a "constant THC" model, which assumes that THC consumption per use day did not change over the period (meaning that the average weight of marijuana consumed per use day decreased). This contrasts with the expenditures series presented above: a "constant grams" series, which assumes that the amount of marijuana consumed in a use day did not change over the decade (meaning that average THC consumption per use day increased). The two series are compared in Figure 5.8, and summary details are provided in Table 5.2. (The rows of Table 5.2 for 2000–2003 are shaded to remind the reader of the limited comparability with the other years.) As potency has been rising over the course of the decade, the trend in expenditures increases much less sharply in the "constant THC" series, only to $26 billion instead of $41 billion.

Table 5.2. Summary of Marijuana Expenditure Results

Year	Price per Gram ($2010)	Population-Adjusted Users	Weight Consumed (MT)	Constant Grams/Day ($2010 Billions)	Average Potency (percent THC)	Constant THC/Day ($2010 Billions)
2000	7.14	16,066,109	3,024	$21.58	5.2	$21.58
2001	6.95	17,746,866	3,479	$24.16	5.8	$21.76
2002	7.48	19,934,738	3,959	$29.60	6.3	$24.59
2003	7.49	19,965,979	3,979	$29.79	6.2	$25.24
2004	7.50	20,572,233	4,198	$31.47	6.7	$24.62
2005	7.16	20,196,226	4,123	$29.53	6.9	$22.37
2006	6.98	20,759,713	4,265	$29.79	7.3	$21.27
2007	7.09	19,946,279	4,264	$30.23	7.9	$19.88
2008	6.72	21,531,816	4,716	$31.68	8.1	$20.48
2009	6.99	23,202,742	5,060	$35.36	7.8	$23.76
2010	7.11	24,487,929	5,734	$40.80	8.1	$26.40

Note: The 2000–2003 marijuana estimates are not perfectly comparable to the later years because of changes in survey questions and methods.

On the other hand, the "constant THC" series may overstate this effect. Even if people would keep THC consumption constant when potency rose and THC prices remained the same, real prices per unit of THC were actually falling. Figure 5.9 shows the trends assuming different levels of the conditional price elasticity of THC demand, from 0.0 to –0.2. The elasticity of 0.0 corresponds to the constant THC scenario. The other two lines show the result of increasing THC consumption per use day in response to the decline in its inflation-adjusted price. Though we can't pinpoint the price elasticity of demand, studies have suggested it is likely to be in the –0.1 to –0.2 range (Dave, 2008; Gallet, 2013). So the effect of considering elasticity in the expenditure estimate is nontrivial, on the order of 5-10 percent.

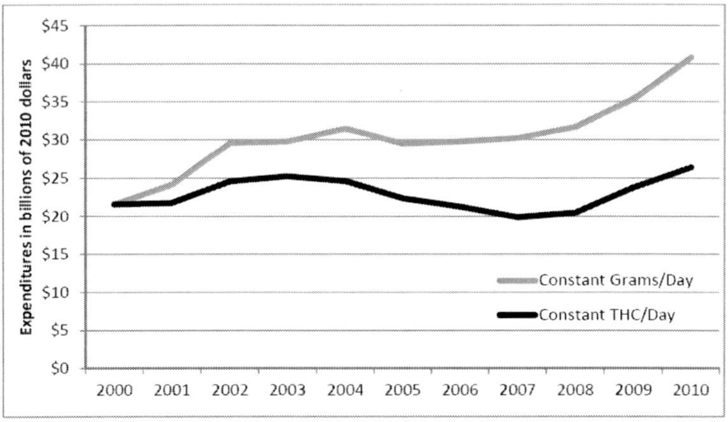

Note: The 2000–2003 marijuana estimates are not perfectly comparable to the later years because of changes in survey questions and methods.

Figure 5.8. Two Different User Responses to Changing Potency. (middle estimates, in billions of 2010 dollars).

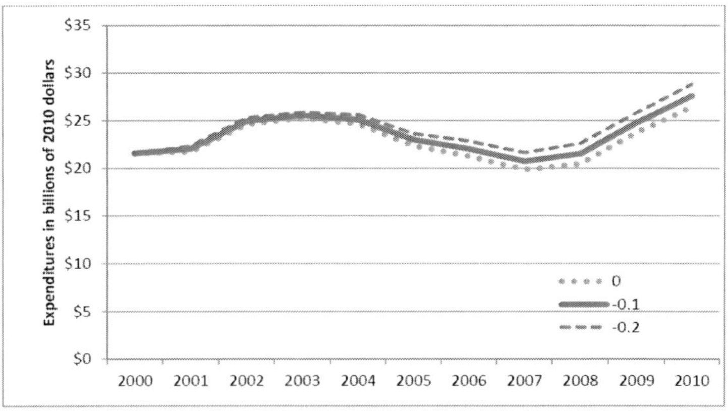

Note: The 2000–2003 marijuana estimates are not perfectly comparable to the later years because of changes in survey questions and methods.

Figure 5.9. Variation in Expenditure Trends, Conditional Price Elasticity of Demand. (middle estimates, in billions of 2010 dollars).

5.4. Comparison with Previous Estimates

This section compares the results presented herein with the results offered in the previous version of this report (ONDCP, 2012c), and offers explanations of the notable differences. Figure 5.10 plots our two estimates of past month users with the baseline estimates from the previous version of this report. The previous estimate and our NSDUH-adjusted estimate yield similar levels and trends.

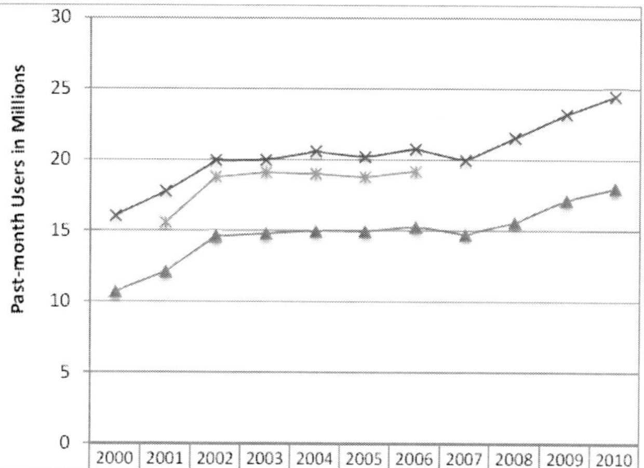

	2000	2001	2002	2003	2004	2005	2006	2007	2008	2009	2010
NSDUH-Raw	10.7	12.1	14.6	14.8	15.0	14.9	15.3	14.7	15.6	17.2	18.0
NSDUH-Adj	16.1	17.7	19.9	20.0	20.6	20.2	20.8	19.9	21.5	23.2	24.5
ONDCP (2012)-NSDUH		15.6	18.8	19.1	19.0	18.8	19.2				

Note: The 2000-2003 marijuana estimates are not perfectly comparable to the later years because of changes in survey questions and methods.

Figure 5.10. Past-Month Marijuana Users, 2000–2010 (in millions).

The previous report estimated that total marijuana expenditures, estimated from NSDUH responses regarding amount spent on marijuana, grew by 46 percent from $25 billion to $36 billion between 2001 and 2002, driven perhaps by a 40-percent increase in the observed price of marijuana in that year (Fries et al., 2008)—or by the difference in NHSDA (pre-2002) and NSDUH (2002 and later) methodology. After that, expenditures (and unit price) show no clear trend, as is apparent from Figure 5.11.

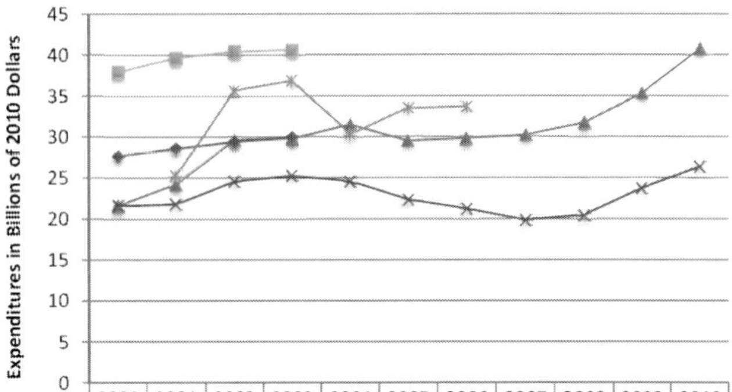

	2000	2001	2002	2003	2004	2005	2006	2007	2008	2009	2010
Constant Grams	22	24	30	30	31	30	30	30	32	35	41
Constant THC	22	22	25	25	25	22	21	20	20	24	26
ONDCP (2012)-Low	28	29	29	30							
ONDCP (2012)-NSDUH		25	36	37	30	34	34				
ONDCP (2012)-High	38	40	40	41							

Note: The 2000–2003 marijuana estimates are not perfectly comparable to the later years because of changes in survey questions and methods.

Figure 5.11. Marijuana Expenditures, 2000–2010 (in billions of 2010 dollars).

The current expenditure estimate, calculated by combining the population-adjusted estimates of consumption with NSDUH-based estimates of marijuana prices, is generally lower than all of the earlier estimates, and also varies more gradually.

We believe the current estimate more accurately reflect expenditures because not only do we incorporate a broader range of price information into our analysis (see Technical Report Section 6.4), we also avoid the assumption that the most recent purchases are representative of all purchases (see Technical Report Section 6.1).

The previous version of this report estimated that overall consumption wavered between 4,500 and 5,000 MTs between 2001 and 2006. As is illustrated in Figure 5.12, our middle estimate is somewhat similar to that earlier NSDUH-based estimate in both trend and level, except that the trend in the previous version decreased about 15 percent from 2004 to 2006; for that period we show no change in consumption.

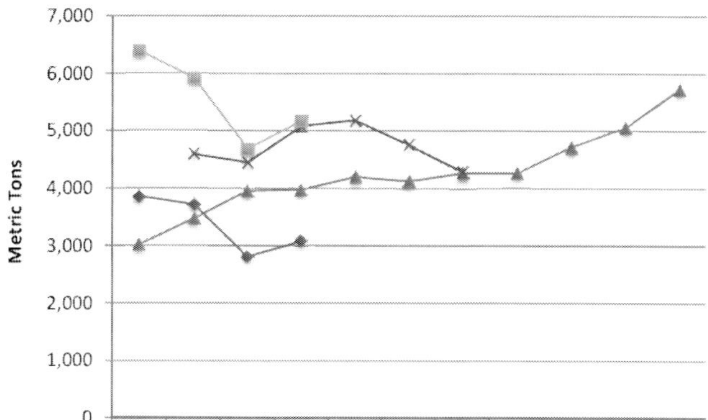

	2000	2001	2002	2003	2004	2005	2006	2007	2008	2009	2010
Middle estimate	3,024	3,479	3,959	3,979	4,198	4,123	4,265	4,264	4,716	5,060	5,734
ONDCP (2012)-Low	3,862	3,723	2,813	3,083							
ONDCP (2012)-NSDUH		4,595	4,453	5,082	5,182	4,750	4,285				
ONDCP (2012)-High	6,394	5,925	4,688	5,177							

Figure 5.12. Marijuana Consumption, 2000–2010 (in MTs).

6. Polydrug Use

6.1. Introduction

Although it is common to hear reference to "cocaine users" or "heroin users," in truth, many people are polydrug users, meaning they consume more than one substance.[19] For example, of the 1,823,006 records in the 2010 TEDS-A database on treatment admissions, more than half (1,012,233, or 56 percent) involved a secondary, not just a primary, substance of abuse. Likewise, of the 20.8 million NSDUH respondents reporting use of an illegal drug other than marijuana in the past year, just over half also reported using marijuana. Polydrug use may even be the norm among frequent users; regular heroin and amphetamine users can average as many as five or six different drugs consumed within the preceding six months (Darke and Hall, 1995). Polydrug use poses a variety of problems, including overdose via drug interactions (Coffin et al., 2003).

However, we show here that most demand for the "big three" expensive illegal drugs in the United States (i.e., cocaine/crack, heroin, and methamphetamine) can be reasonably understood from a single drug perspective. In particular, most frequent users of any one of those drugs are not simultaneously frequent users of either of the other two. This absence of overlap does ***not*** extend to marijuana.

6.2. Methodology and Results

To estimate the level of polydrug use, we rely on NSDUH and ADAM. Combining data from nine NSDUH surveys (2002–2010) yields a total of 500,914 respondents, so even the heaviest use categories include a fair number of respondents.

6.2.1. Results from the National Survey on Drug Use and Health

Results are stated in terms of the simple average across the nine survey years of the sampling-weighted estimates and the (unweighted) sum of all respondents over the nine surveys.

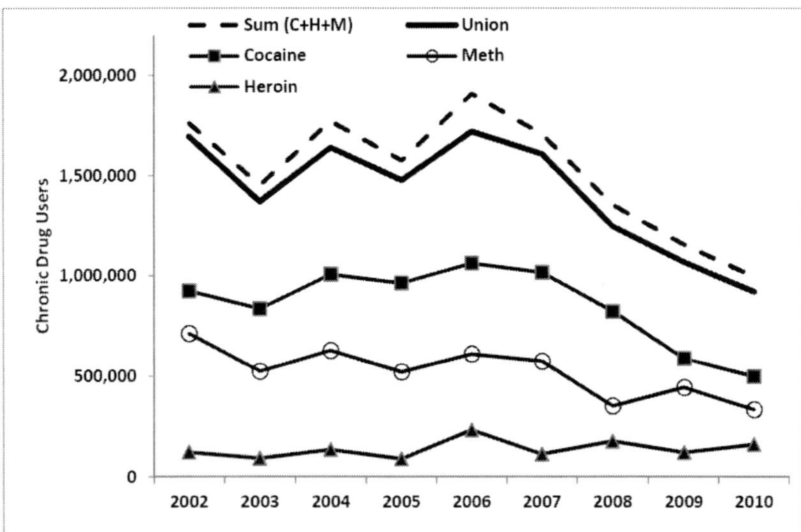

Note: Solid line shows how close their union (number of CDUs of one or more of the substances) is to the sum.

Figure 6.1. Number of Chronic Users of Cocaine, Heroin, and Meth (based on NSDUH).

Adding across all nine surveys, 3,390 NSDUH respondents met the criteria for chronic use of a "big three" drug. Adding the separate counts of chronic users of cocaine, heroin, and meth yields a total of 3,653. That is, the number of respondents who were CDUs (people who used four or more times in the past month) for any one of the drugs is 92.8 percent of the number obtained by summing the number of chronic users of each drug separately. The proportion is nearly the same when factoring in the sampling weights: The number in the union (1,415,354) was 93.2 percent as large as the sum (1,519,353).

This proportion has been stable over time (see Figure 6.1), even though there has been a steep decline in chronic cocaine use and changes in NSDUH questions concerning meth. In all years, the overall number of CDUs was 90–96 percent of the sum of the three single-drug CDU counts. Visually, this means the solid black line (indicating the union) was within 5–10 percent of the dashed line indicating the sum.

6.2.2. Results from the Arrestee Drug Abuse Monitoring Program

ADAM data likewise find some overlap among ***frequent*** users of these three substances, but not a lot. The emphasis on frequent is important. Many daily users of one of the three drugs also used another of the three at some point in the last year, but relatively few used another hard drug more than occasionally.

Consider first the overlap between cocaine (including crack) and heroin, the pair that has the greatest overlap.[20]

The ADAM-I (2000–2003) data include 23,881 male and female respondents who reported past-month use of cocaine and/or heroin.[21] Most (20,099, or 84 percent) reported using just one or the other drug; fewer than one in six used both in the past month. However, the overlap was asymmetric. About two-thirds (64 percent) of past-month heroin users had also used cocaine in the same period (1/4 * 2/3 = 1/6), but only about one in six of those who had used cocaine (17 percent) also used heroin.

The same pattern holds among the 8,026 respondents who used one or more of the drugs on a daily/near-daily basis (more than 20 times per month). Almost two-thirds of the daily/near-daily heroin users (2,068 of 3,165, or 65 percent) also reported any past-month cocaine use, whereas only about one-quarter (1,587 of 5,957, or 27 percent) of the daily/near daily cocaine users also reported heroin use. If one ignores occasional use of the second drug (meaning fewer than four days in the past month), those proportions shrink to 55 percent and 23 percent, respectively.

Table 6.1 reports these proportions for all pairs of the three hard drugs. The third column shows results for cocaine vis a vis the sum of heroin and meth. There is little overlap between heroin and meth, so this combination provides a sense of polydrug use overall, without the complexity of considering three-way permutations (e.g., P{ use drug A | used drug B daily and C not more than three times }, etc.)

Table 6.1. Extent of Polydrug Use Reported in ADAM-I (by percentage)

Drug A	Cocaine	Cocaine	Cocaine	Meth	Meth	Heroin
Drug B	Heroin	Meth	Meth + Heroin	Heroin	Cocaine + Heroin	Cocaine + Meth
P{ just one | A or B }	84	91	82	94	90	87
P{ A | B }	64	24	35	18	13	13
P{ B | A }	17	13	27	9	26	70
P{ A | Daily B }	65	19	42	12	12	20
P{ B | Daily A }	27	12	33	8	22	68
P{ A 4+ times/mo. | Daily B }	55	8	32	7	6	16
P{ B 4+ times/mo. | Daily A }	23	5	25	4	11	58
P{ A 4+ times/mo. | B 4+ times/mo. }	54	11	26	9	6	13
P{ B 4+ times/mo. | A 4+ times/mo. }	18	6	22	5	13	58

Table 6.2 expresses the overlaps in terms of number of CDUs. It shows that adding the numbers of drug-specific CDUs (14,266 + 4,646 + 7,934 = 26,846) would overstate the actual number of CDUs (23,438) by about 15 percent. Figure 6.2 shows the overlap among CDU with a Venn diagram. Thus there is slightly more polydrug use among ADAM than NSDUH respondents, but the difference is not substantial.

ADAM-II has more recent data, but for a smaller number of counties. We replicate the analysis for the ADAM-II cities for both the same years (2000–2003) and with newer data (from 2007–2010) and obtain substantially similar results. Indeed, as Table 6.3 shows, if anything there was perhaps even less indication of polydrug use in 2007-2010.

Table 6.2. ADAM-I Data Suggest the Number of Hard-Drug CDUs is Approximately 7/8th as Large as the Naïve Estimate Obtained by Adding the Numbers of Those Who Use Each Drug Chronically

Chronic Cocaine Use?	Chronic Heroin Use?	Chronic Meth Use?	# of ADAM-I Respondents
Yes	Yes	Yes	456
Yes	Yes	No	2,062
Yes	No	Yes	383
Yes	No	No	11,365
No	Yes	Yes	51
No	Yes	No	2,077
No	No	Yes	7,044
No	No	No	
		# of Cocaine CDUs	14,266
		# of Heroin CDUs	4,646
		# of Meth CDUs	7,934
		Sum of 3 #'s of CDUs	26,846
		Actual Total # of CDUs	23,438
		Naïve / Actual Estimate	**1.145**

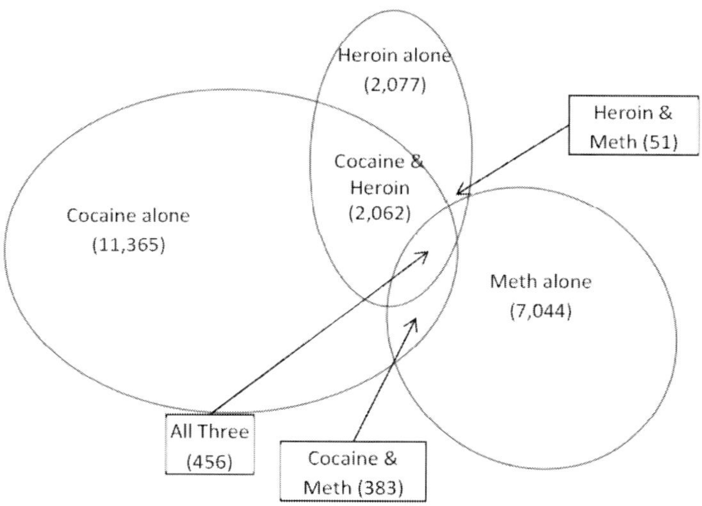

Figure 6.2. Overlap Among ADAM Respondents Using Cocaine/Crack, Heroin, or Meth Four or More Times per Month.

Table 6.3. Contrasting Polydrug Use in ADAM-II counties in 2000-2003 vs. 2007-2010

Drug A	Cocaine	Cocaine	Cocaine	Cocaine
Drug B	Heroin	Heroin	Meth	Meth
Years	2000-2003	2007-2010	2000-2003	2007-2010
P{ just one | A or B }	81	86	94	95
P{ A | B }	63	55	27	21
P{ B | A }	21	16	7	7
P{ A | Daily B }	63	54	18	13
P{ B | Daily A }	30	20	6	6
P{ A 4+ times/mo. | Daily B }	55	42	8	7
P{ B 4+ times/mo. | Daily A }	26	17	2	3

Table 6.4 shows that except for heroin, polydrug use is also the exception when counting days-ofuse, rather than users. Most use of cocaine and methamphetamine (77 percent and 88 percent of use days, respectively in ADAM-I) is by people who reported using no other hard drug more than 3 times in the past month. The corresponding proportion for heroin is lower.

Table 6.4. Proportion of Use Days for Drug by People Who Report Using Other Hard Drugs (by Percentage)

		Frequency of use of other hard drug(s)		
Data Source	Drug	< 4 days per month	4-20 days per month	21+ days per month
ADAM-I Cities	Heroin	42	24	34
	Meth	88	6	6
	Cocaine	77	7	16
ADAM-II 2000-2003	Heroin	44	24	32
	Meth	85	7	8
	Cocaine	76	6	18
ADAM-II 2007-2010	Heroin	53	23	23
	Meth	87	7	6
	Cocaine	82	6	12

6.3. Discussion

The question investigated here is how much overlap there is among chronic users with regard to the "big three" expensive illegal drugs (i.e., cocaine/crack, heroin, methamphetamine). Since chronic users dominate consumption, this is essentially the same as asking whether demand for these substances comes primarily from a single pool of polydrug users, or from three more or less distinct populations who (at least at the moment) have a single primary drug of choice.

The key finding is that the total number of chronic users of these substances is only modestly smaller than the total obtained by adding the number of chronic users of heroin to the number of chronic users of meth and the number of chronic users of cocaine or crack. In other words, there is relatively little overlap among the populations, so the whole is not much less than the sum of its parts.

Among household survey respondents, the total is about 93 percent of the sum of the parts. Among arrestees, the proportion is slightly lower, closer to 88 percent. Assuming the overall market can be thought of as intermediate between these groups, the true overall figure might be that the number of CDUs is about 90 percent of the sum of the three drug-specific CDU counts.

This is at odds with the conventional wisdom that polydrug use is the norm, although others have made similar observations in the past. For example, Brecht et al. (2003) argue that one can classify drug users as primary heroin, cocaine, or meth abusers even if they sometimes use another of those substances on the side.

We do not want to overstate the finding. It applies ***among*** the big three expensive drugs, but it is common for frequent users of one of these substances to also use alcohol and or marijuana frequently. It applies to amounts of use (and, similarly, demand), not numbers of users. The majority of ADAM respondents who reported daily use of one of the "big three" drugs also reported having used at least one other such drug at some point in their lifetime. The majority of daily heroin users (but not of daily cocaine or methamphetamine users), had even used another of the three drugs within the last year.[22] So in an expansive sense, arrestees who use daily are mostly polydrug users; but that does not mean they are deeply involved currently in the use of more than one of the "big three" drugs.

Therefore, in terms of counting the number of chronic users of the "big three" (i.e., four or more times in the previous month), the sum of users in each group is a good approximation of the number of chronic users of any one.

While certainly there is some overlap, if one adds the numbers of people who use each drug chronically, that sum is only modestly greater than the number of people who use one or more of these drugs with such frequency; that is, the overlap is rather modest. In other words, the number of chronic users of cocaine/crack or heroin or methamphetamine is approximated by adding the number of chronic users of cocaine/crack to the number of chronic users of heroin and to the number of chronic users of methamphetamine. The same cannot be said when marijuana is considered—but as we've already argued, there is little relevance to the concept of a user of marijuana or cocaine/crack or heroin or methamphetamine because so many people who use other drugs also use marijuana.

More generally, one can think of the problem with wholly illicit drugs (as opposed to diverted pharmaceuticals or alcohol, and ignoring marijuana) as being the sum of the problems associated with cocaine/crack, with heroin, and with methamphetamine.

7. Comparing Drug Consumption Estimates with Supply Indicators

Sections Four and Five present two different approaches for estimating illicit drug consumption.[23] For marijuana, we multiply use days by the average amount consumed per use day, and then multiply that number by the number of users.[24] For the other drugs, we divide total expenditures by the average amount spent per pure gram purchased. With both approaches, we describe the uncertainty surrounding these figures, and we attempt to be transparent about the most consequential assumptions that underlie them.

Table 7.1 presents our middle, lower, and higher consumption estimates. The middle figures could also be termed best estimates. The lower and higher ends of the range are meant to give some sense of the uncertainty, but they have a very specific and nuanced meaning that is vulnerable to misinterpretation. For cocaine, heroin, and meth, they reflect only one source of uncertainty: the 95- percent confidence interval surrounding the share of adult male arrest events involving a positive drug test. For marijuana expenditures and consumption, the lower range is based on NSDUH estimates with no adjustment for underreporting, and the higher range multiplies this value by two. Since there are many other sources of uncertainty, readers should not consider these as lower or upper bounds or as 95-percent confidence intervals.

Table 7.1. Consumption of Illegal Drugs, 2000–2010 (in pure MTs, except marijuana)

Drug	Estimate	2000	2001	2002	2003	2004	2005	2006	2007	2008	2009	2010
Cocaine	Middle	292	258	278	278	324	327	322	282	200	161	145
	Lower-Higher	193–440	175–386	183–428	182–428	209–500	211–501	208–494	182–431	132–302	105–248	92–227
Heroin	Middle	22	25	22	23	23	22	22	24	26	27	24
	Lower-Higher	11–37	13–41	12–37	12–38	12–37	12–36	12–36	13–39	14–42	15–45	13–40
Marijuana[a] (1000 MT)	Middle	3.0	3.5	4.0	4.0	4.2	4.1	4.3	4.3	4.7	5.1	5.7
	Lower-Higher	2.0–3.9	2.3–4.7	2.9–5.7	2.9–5.8	3.0–6.1	3.1–6.1	3.1–6.2	3.1–6.2	3.4–6.8	3.8–7.5	4.2–8.4
Meth	Middle	20	26	41	48	61	85	58	54	39	40	42
	Lower-Higher	8–43	11–49	20–70	24–77	32–95	47–127	32–88	28–83	20–63	19–66	19–71

Notes: The lower and higher ends of the range are meant to give some sense of the uncertainty, but they have a very specific and nuanced meaning that is vulnerable to misinterpretation. Please see text.

[a] The 2000 and 2001 estimates are not perfectly comparable to the later years, as a consequence of the differences between NHSDA (2001 and earlier) and NSDUH (2002 and later).

These two "demand-side" approaches are not the only way to estimate availability. As explained in Section One, there are also "supply-side" methods that focus on the amount of drugs produced (net of seizures and other removals from the market). This Section will not calculate supply-based estimates, but will compare our results with various supply-side indicators. Similar to the structure of the document, we begin with cocaine, heroin, and methamphetamine, and then examine the estimates for marijuana.

7.1. Cocaine

More effort has been made to develop systematic estimates of production, shipment, and amounts available for consumption for cocaine than for any other drug. Enormous progress has been made in understanding the basic parameters of the global cocaine supply system.

For cocaine there is a relatively elaborate set of supply indicators and models to assess the amounts "available for consumption" in the United States annually. This section focuses on three supply-based indictors:

- U.S. estimates of Colombian cocaine production
- estimates of cocaine border seizures
- cocaine availability estimates based on the Interagency Assessment of Cocaine Movement (IACM).

7.1.1. U.S. Estimates of Colombian Cocaine Production

Data from the DEA's Cocaine Signature Program suggest that for most of the decade, more than 90 percent of the cocaine seized and tested by DEA in the United States was processed from coca cultivated in Colombia (DEA, 2003; UNODC, 2011). Thus, one supply-side indicator of the U.S. cocaine market is the estimated quantity of coca cultivated in Colombia. Of course, this is an imperfect measure; Americans consume some non-Colombian cocaine, and some Colombian-produced cocaine is consumed in other countries. The latter has become more relevant over time as cocaine consumption has increased outside of the United States, especially in Europe (UNODC, 2010).

Nevertheless, production figures are still relevant, even if much less so than in the past when the United States dominated global cocaine consumption. Figure 7.1 presents data from the CIA's Crime and Narcotics Center (CNC) and the Colombian government about coca cultivation, eradication, and potential production in Colombia. The estimates for potential production fluctuate from 2000 to 2006, then steadily decline by almost 50 percent through 2010. Hectares of land believed to be used for coca cultivation also substantially decreased in the second half of the decade.

There is tremendous uncertainty surrounding these figures Indeed the previous version of this report argues: "The confidence interval is so wide that estimates from any year are not very useful. It seems quixotic to make much of year-by-year changes in potential production regardless of whether the source is CNC or UNODC" (ONDCP, 2012c, 46). However, the measured decline from 2005 to 2010 is so large that it seems likely that there has, indeed, been a reduction in Colombian production.

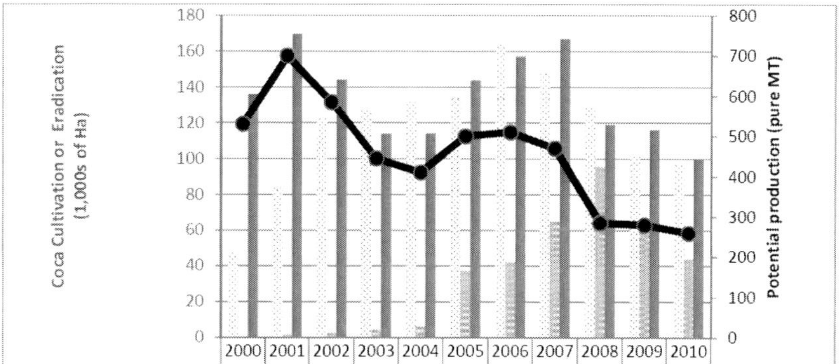

	2000	2001	2002	2003	2004	2005	2006	2007	2008	2009	2010
Aerial Spray	47	84	123	127	132	134	164	148	130	102	98
Manual Erad		2	3	4	6	38	42	65	96	61	44
Cultivation	136	170	144	114	114	144	157	167	119	116	100
Potential Pure Prod	530	700	585	445	410	500	510	470	285	280	260

Figure 7.1. Colombian Trends in Coca Cultivation, Eradication, and Cocaine Production, 2000–2010.

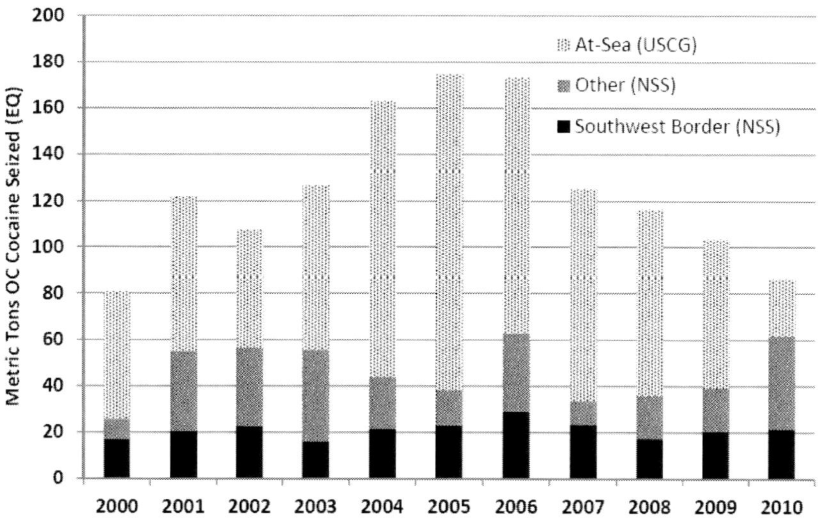

Source: National Seizure System (NSS), EPIC, extracted 3/15/2013, and US Coast Guard.

Figure 7.2. Cocaine Seizures from the Southwest Border, the Rest of the United States, and At-Sea, 2000–2010.

7.1.2. Estimates of Cocaine Seizures

The bulk of reports in the National Seizure System (NSS) are from federal law enforcement, but some are from participating state and local law enforcement. Although not inclusive of all law enforcement drug-seizure reporting, the NSS is the most complete database available, and it seems plausible that most large seizures get into it.[25] Figure 7.2 presents data on seizures since 2000, and distinguishes among locations [southwest border, at-sea, other]. Total cocaine seizures fell by one half between 2006 and 2010, from about 160 tons to about 80 tons, at export level purity.

7.1.3. Interagency Assessment of Cocaine Movement (IACM)

The IACM is an annual report intended to advise policymakers and resource planners whose responsibilities involve detecting, monitoring, and interdicting illicit drug shipments. The Defense Intelligence Agency is the Executive Agent for IACM, and other participants include the CNC; the Coast Guard; CBP; DEA; Joint Interagency Task Force South (JIATF-South); JIATF-West; the Department of Homeland Security; the El Paso Intelligence Center; the National Security Agency; the Office of Naval Intelligence; the State Department; the U.S. Southern Command, and United Kingdom liaison partners (GAO, 2005). The annual report uses the aforementioned data about potential production estimates, information about movement and seizures captured in the Consolidated Counterdrug Database (CCDB), and estimates of cocaine consumption, as well as information from a number of other sources.

> The Consolidated Counterdrug Database (CCDB) is a comprehensive data collection effort that captures the details surrounding cocaine movement events submitted by U.S. and foreign counterdrug agencies. International and interagency partners gather quarterly to review all reported interdiction cases and vet the information for input into the database.
>
> They also revise, de-conflict, and validate data on overall counterdrug performance, trafficking trends, and regional cocaine flow (Stavridis, 2010).

ONDCP publishes a summary of the report highlights under the title "***Cocaine Smuggling in Year X.***" Figure 7.3 is the summary figure from ***Cocaine Smuggling in Year 2010*** (ONDCP, 2012a). All of these figures are presented not in MTs, but in terms of export quality (EQ), which represents the purity of cocaine departing South America.

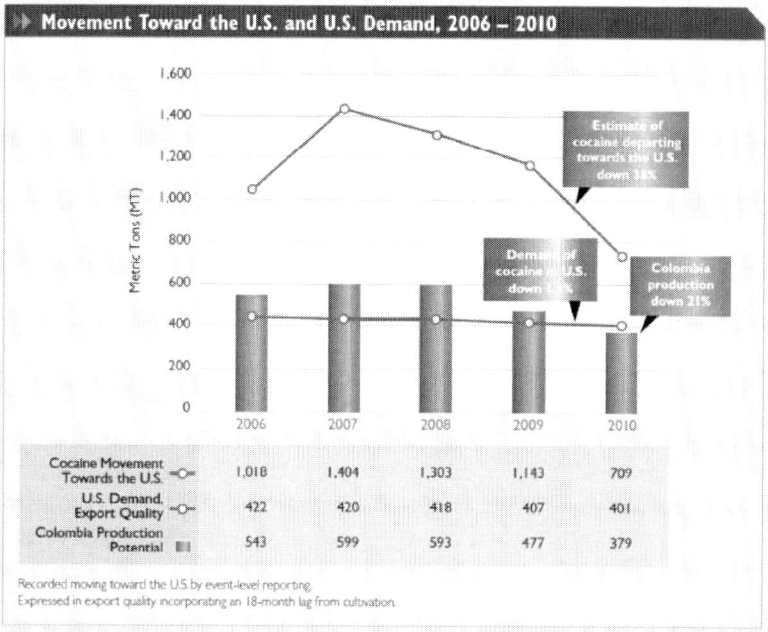

Source: Reproduced from a document prepared for ONDCP (ONDCP, 2012a). The rest of this section addresses these three quantities of interest.

Figure 7.3. Estimates from *Cocaine Smuggling in Year 2010* (purity EQ).

7.1.3.1. Colombian Potential Production

CNC production data in Figure 7.1 suggest that Colombian cocaine production decreased almost 50 percent from 2006 to 2010 (510 pure MTs to 260 pure MTs). The Colombia potential production figures (EQ purity) presented in Figure 7.3 suggest a decrease closer to 30 percent (543 MT EQ to 379 MT EQ; delayed 18 months). The difference in these estimates is well within the margin of error, so the important observation is not their differences, but rather their agreement about a large decrease from 2006 to 2010. What is striking about Figure 7.3 is that the amount reported to be consumed in the United States ***exceeds*** the estimate for potential production in Colombia in 2010 (401 MT EQ vs. 379 MT EQ). While this could be a function of cocaine coming from other sources, this is not consistent with forensic evidence from law enforcement sources; e.g., ***International Narcotics Control Strategy Report*** (INCSR) (Bureau of International Narcotics and Law Enforcement Affairs, 2009).[26] Further, this does not account for the amounts seized on the way to the United States, or consumption in the Transit Zone (Mexico, Central America, Caribbean islands). We look more into these consumption figures in the next section.

7.1.3.2. U.S. Consumption

The demand figures for the United States, as tabulated by the ***Cocaine Smuggling in 2010*** report and shown in Figure 7.3, suggest raw consumption only decreased by 5 percent from 2006 to 2010. This is sharply at odds with a number of indicators suggesting that the number of heavy and occasional users in the United States decreased substantially over this period (See Section Four).

Unclassified passages from the classified 2010 IACM report state that the estimates for the United States are based entirely upon NSDUH and assumptions about daily consumption;[27] however, there is almost universal agreement that NSDUH is not appropriate for estimating the size of the cocaine market (e.g., Brecht et al., 2003; ONDCP, 2001; 2012c). This seems especially problematic when attempting to understand the share of cocaine consumption in the United States attributed to powder versus crack. The extent to which a general-population survey can reasonably reflect national consumption may also vary over the course of a drug epidemic, as the share of consumption that comes from groups that are easier or harder to survey may shift.

A similar methodology largely based on general-population surveys was used to generate consumption estimates for other countries, although different assumptions about quantity consumed were used for three regions: the United States and Canada, western Europe, and the rest of the world). Almost all these areas have far less data available than in the United States, for which consumption estimates have large confidence intervals. Thus, the estimates for individual countries other than the United States should be used with caution. This uncertainty has implications for the cocaine flow estimates discussed in the next section.

7.1.3.3. Cocaine Departing South America for the United States

The cocaine movement data reported in Figure 7.3 suggest that there was an increase in cocaine heading to the United States from South America from 2006 to 2007, followed by a 50-percent decrease from 2007 to 2010. Other reported cocaine flow figures are based on a combination of two estimates (production- and consumption-based estimates). The agencies have gathered increasing evidence that cocaine departing the production areas of South

America may take perhaps as long as two years to reach the retail market in the United States (Ehleringer et al., 2011; Ehleringer et al., 2012). Hence, IACM estimates for the United States incorporate production with an 18-month lag to current "removals" this year; removals is the sum of consumption, seizures, and "other losses" (e.g., shipments dumped at sea).

Although not displayed in this particular chart or document, there is a lot of uncertainty surrounding these estimates. To get a better understanding, Figure 7.4 presents a figure from ***Cocaine Smuggling in 2007*** (ONDCP, 2008). The 2007 "common range" of 545–707 MTs appears to be pulled from two sources: the "higher confidence" figure of the movement-based estimate (545 MTs) and upper bound of the consumption-based estimate (707 MTs). In other words, this is not a range, let alone a confidence interval in the conventional sense; it is merely the juxtaposition of two separate estimates that differ by about 25 percent. Furthermore, the note to the table reports that "About 626 metric tons of cocaine departed from South America toward the United States. . ."; presumably the 626 MTs was generated by taking the midpoint of the 545–707 MTs.

Source: Reproduced from *Cocaine Smuggling in 2007* (ONDCP, 2008).

Figure 7.4. Estimates of Cocaine Flow from *Cocaine Smuggling in Year 2007* (EQ).

To illustrate the uncertainty surrounding the movement-based figures, Figure 7.5 displays how the "higher confidence" and "lower confidence" figures fluctuated from 2006–2009 (***Cocaine Smuggling in 2009***; ONDCP, 2010). Movements documented by the CCDB have three levels of certainty: confirmed (seizures), substantiated (visual or corroborating information), and suspect (lowest confidence). The "higher confidence" estimates include those that are confirmed or substantiated. The ratio of lower to higher confidence increased from 2:1 in 2006 (1,032/518) to nearly 3:1 in 2009 (1,149/393). While the higher confidence estimate decreased by almost 25 percent from 2006 to 2009; the lower confidence estimate actually increased by slightly more than 10 percent over this period.

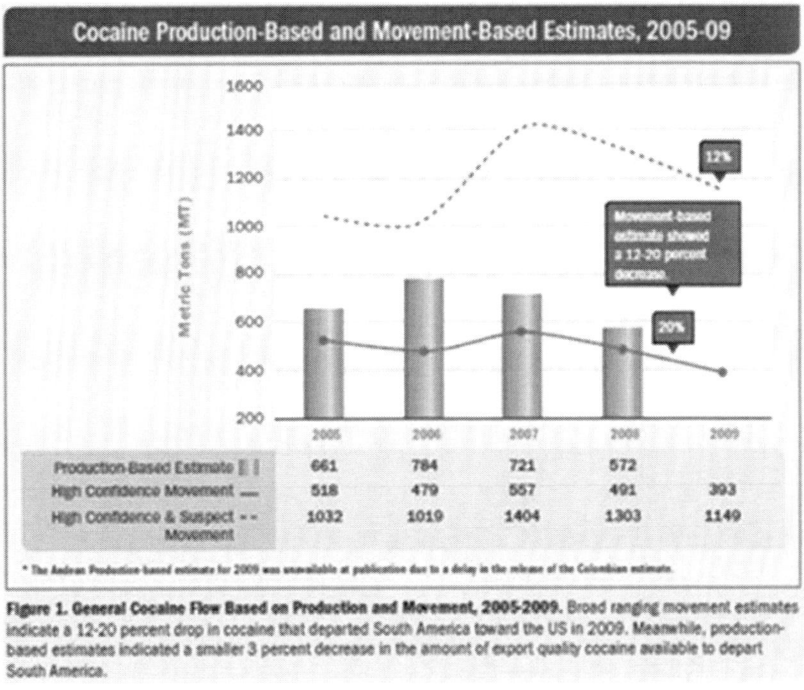

Figure 7.5. Estimates of Cocaine Flow from *Cocaine Smuggling in Year 2009* (EQ).

7.1.4. Comparison with Consumption Estimates

Multiple indicators on the demand and supply side all point to a roughly 50-percent decline over the relatively short time between 2006 and 2010. Our consumption results suggest that the number of pure MTs of cocaine consumed in the United States decreased by roughly half over the decade, with most of the decrease occurring after 2006.[28] CNC estimates of pure potential production in Colombia likewise decreased by about half after 2006. Similarly, trend data from ***Cocaine Smuggling in 2010*** show a large increase in cocaine movements from 2006–2007, followed by nearly a 50-percent drop from 2007 to 2010. Finally, retail powder cocaine purity fell in the United States over this period, which is consistent with a constrained supply (from 74 percent to 52 percent, unpublished data from IDA published in ONDCP, 2013a, Table 62).

7.2. Heroin

Global opium production has been dominated by Afghanistan since the mid-1990s (Bureau of International Narcotics and Law Enforcement Affairs, 2013). Although Afghanistan produces the vast majority of the world's illicit opiates, only limited quantities of heroin seized and tested in American cities are of Afghan origin. Analyses of seizures in the United States suggest that about 95 percent comes from South American—most likely Colombia and Mexico. Moreover, U.S. consumption is believed to account for the vast majority of production from these two countries. Thus, the following analysis focuses exclusively on Latin American heroin production and exports.

Figure 7.6 presents data justifying this focus. The DEA's Heroin Signature Program (HSP) reports the results of analyses of a sample of primarily large seizures in the United States, identifying the country of origin. In addition, there are analyses of the origins of undercover retail purchases made as part of the Heroin Domestic Monitoring Program (DMP) in approximately 25 cities.[29] In most cities, the DMP goal is to make 40 retail purchases spread out over the four quarters of the year— New York City aims to make 80 purchases each year; and seven smaller cities, just 20 each.

As shown in Figure 7.6, Asia (mostly Afghanistan and Myanmar) accounted for the majority of the HSP analyzed seizures, by weight, for most of the years from 1980 to 1994. Since 1998, the share for Asia has never been more than 15 percent and often much less; in recent years, there have been no seizures or purchases from Southeast Asia. The DMP data shown in Figure 7.7 for 1995–2010 are broadly consistent in showing the domination of Mexico and Colombia and the total absence of Southeast Asian heroin in recent years. There are a few large differences, however. For example, in 2003, the Mexican share in the HSP is only 3 percent—whereas in DMP, samples originating from Mexico account for 39 percent of the total.

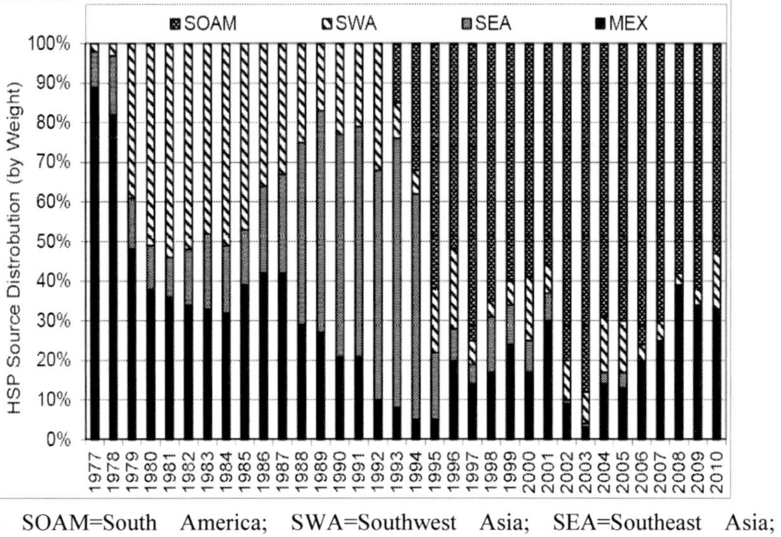

Note: SOAM=South America; SWA=Southwest Asia; SEA=Southeast Asia; MEX=Mexico.

Figure 7.6. Source of Heroin Seizures in the United States, 1977–2010.

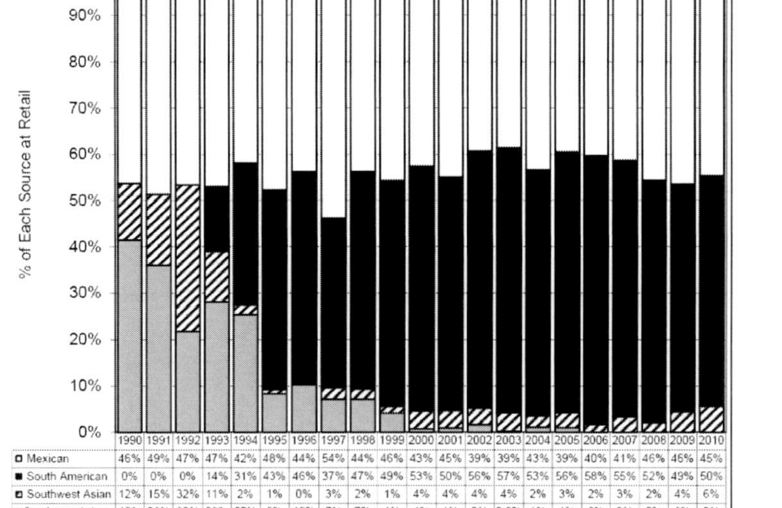

	1990	1991	1992	1993	1994	1995	1996	1997	1998	1999	2000	2001	2002	2003	2004	2005	2006	2007	2008	2009	2010
Mexican	46%	49%	47%	47%	42%	48%	44%	54%	44%	46%	43%	45%	39%	39%	43%	39%	40%	41%	46%	46%	45%
South American	0%	0%	0%	14%	31%	43%	46%	37%	47%	49%	53%	50%	56%	57%	53%	56%	58%	55%	52%	49%	50%
Southwest Asian	12%	15%	32%	11%	2%	1%	0%	3%	2%	1%	4%	4%	4%	4%	2%	3%	2%	3%	2%	4%	6%
Southeast Asian	42%	36%	22%	28%	25%	8%	10%	7%	7%	4%	1%	1%	2%	0.2%	1%	1%	0%	0%	0%	0%	0%

Source: DMP, various years.

Figure 7.7. Source of DMP Purchases, 1990–2010.

Differences between the HSP and DMP are expected because they are based on different samples. Fluctuations in the HSP also may reflect changing trafficking patterns, as well as enforcement priorities. If resources are shifted to the Mexican border, the share of seizures coming from Mexico is likely to increase. A shift to airport inspection and surveillance will likely increase the share of seizures from Colombia, much of which is flown in by body carriers.

Apart from year-to-year shifts, there may be statistical bias in the program (i.e., factors that lead to sustained and systematic differences between the two sources). For example, Mexican smugglers may make more shipments between ports of entry (POEs), compared to the air-shipment dependent Colombian smugglers. If between-POE smuggling is lower risk than POE smuggling, the result will be an overrepresentation of Colombian seizures compared to Colombia's share of imports.

The DMP includes a substantial percentage of samples that are of unknown origin (UNKs); in 2011, there were 197 samples that could not be identified with one of the four sources of origin, amounting to 23.5 percent of the total observations. If, as has been conjectured by the DEA, there are Colombian chemists working with Mexican refiners to produce white heroin from Mexican opium, that might produce a number of UNKs that ought to be classified as Mexican.[30] Since UNK specimens are excluded from the analysis of national shares, that would lead to an under-representation of Mexican heroin.

There is also a marked spatial pattern. When the proportion of DMP observations that are Mexican vs. South American in origin are plotted on a map, the country divides fairly neatly into regions where the two sources dominate: Mexican heroin west of the Mississippi and Colombian east of the Mississippi. It is not the case that there is one homogenous U.S. market, within which there is more or less a consistent proportion in any given city from each source region. Rather, most cities have one dominant source region. The decision about which cities are included in DMP can influence the overall proportion of DMP observations that are from one source region or another.

7.2.1. Heroin Production in Colombia and Mexico

Figure 7.8 presents the CNC estimates of heroin production in Colombia for the period 1999–2010, as published in the State Department's annual INCSR. The figures steadily declined throughout the decade, and it is widely believed that Colombian production was replaced by Mexican production. However, recent methodological changes make it difficult to say anything definitive about heroin availability in the United States over this period. In

2011, the methodological model for both Mexican marijuana and poppy cultivation was revised, which sharply reduced the estimates due to reducing the number of growing seasons from three to two. The U.S. government now recognizes that the previous estimates were inflated. There are no back-cast revised estimates (marijuana and poppy/heroin) for the whole country of Mexico prior to 2011.[31]

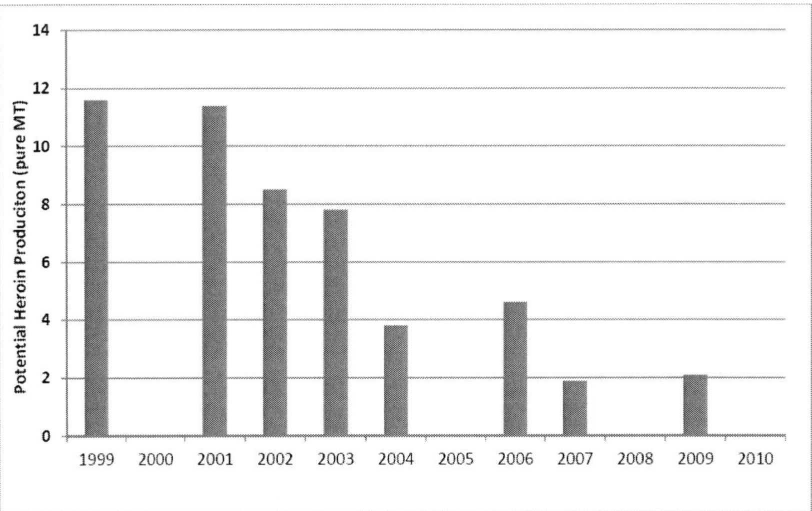

Notes: INCSR 2013: "No estimates in 2005, 2008, 2010, or 2011 due to cloud cover."

Figure 7.8. Estimated Heroin Production in Colombia (MTs), 1999–2010.

But if it is true, this points to a paradox that was extensively analyzed by ONDCP (2012c), covering 2000–2006. If Colombian production has collapsed and Mexican production has soared, how is it possible that both HSP and DMP continue to show roughly the same share of purchased heroin coming from the two countries? For example, Colombia accounted for 49 percent of DMP specimens, and Mexico for 44 percent, in 2009 [32]

One possibility is underestimation of Colombian production. Cultivation estimates are made more difficult by cloud cover, intercropping with licit agriculture, and dispersal of fields. There have been years (such as 2005 and 2008) in which the lack of cloud-free days precluded an estimate of cultivation area, the first step in the estimation procedure. There have been shifts in production method data that have required back-casting adjustments to estimates. Still, none of this suggests the possibility that Colombian heroin production has expanded or is comparable to the recent figures for Mexican production. The INCSR for 2012 reports heroin seizure levels in Colombia in recent years that are consistent with production levels that are modestly lower than previously. For 2007–2010, the total reported seizures of heroin in Colombia were 2.35 tons; in the previous four years, the total was 2.8 tons. This is, of course, a much smaller decline than in the estimated production levels, but still does not point to production in Colombia that might compare with that estimated for Mexico.

Another potential source of inconsistency lies in the forensic signature analysis itself. The HSP and DMP depend on obtaining background intelligence, investigative details, and authentic specimens from each unique production type. An authentic specimen is an acquisition with a known source country. Heroin processing classifications result from differences in starting material and processing methods. Heroin classifications are contingent upon consistent starting material from a source country being processed via consistent means. If either the starting material or the synthetic route were to be varied, the analytical results could result in an unknown classification. If a source country begins to produce heroin specimens that are forensically similar to an existing production method in a different country, but few or no authentics are collected from the new production method, the signature trends from the HSP's or DMP's classified sample pools are unlikely to indicate it. If Mexican heroin refiners have switched to the use of chemicals and methods that previously have characterized refining in Colombia, then DMP or HSP will overestimate the share that comes from Colombia.

Estimates of heroin consumption in Latin America have no known provenance; they must be very uncertain given the slight availability of data on prevalence and consumption.[33] However, no government or analyst claims that there is a substantial market specifically for heroin or heroin-derived products in Latin American countries. For example, the 2011 ***World Drug Report***, discussing 2009, states, "In the Americas, the United States of America dominated heroin consumption" (UNODC, 2011, p. 46). The Mexican ***Evaluation of Progress in Drug Control 2007–2009***, produced under the Mutual Evaluation Mechanism of the Organization of American States, presents a variety of indicators of consumption. None shows much domestic heroin consumption, though the indicators are not particularly strong.[34] Some South American countries have a substantial narcotics problem, but the narcotics are diverted pharmaceuticals, rather than opium-based products.

7.2.2. Heroin Seizures

There is some evidence for an increase in imports from Mexico in the form of higher seizures of heroin at the U.S. border with Mexico. Mexican heroin enters via the southwest border; much of the Colombian heroin enters without going through Mexico (in contrast to cocaine). Southwest border seizures averaged 350 kilograms annually for the period 2001–2005. They have averaged 830 kilograms in the most recent three years 2008–2010, and show a sharp increase during those three years, as indicated in Figure 7.9. The seizures away from the southwest border show a very different pattern, declining by three quarters through 2009; 2010 saw an increase but still to a level less than half of that in 2001. Whereas southwest border seizures accounted for only one-sixth of total Arrival Zone seizures in 2001, they account for more than 55 percent by 2010. That said, the 2010 total (3,291 kilograms) is only 15 percent higher than the 2002 figure (2,898 in 2002).

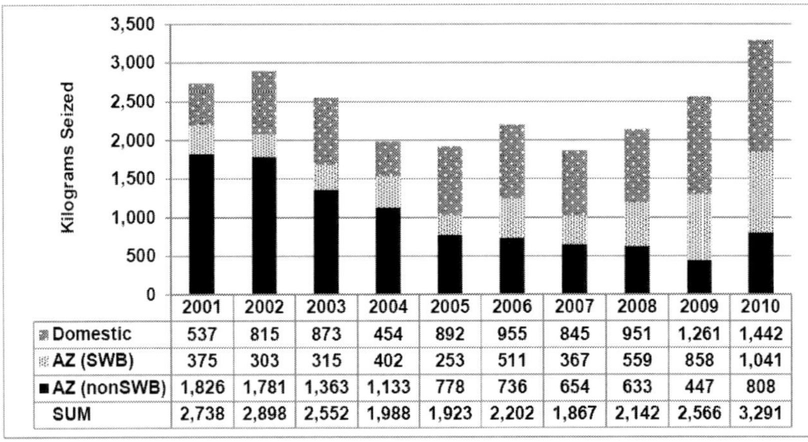

	2001	2002	2003	2004	2005	2006	2007	2008	2009	2010
Domestic	537	815	873	454	892	955	845	951	1,261	1,442
AZ (SWB)	375	303	315	402	253	511	367	559	858	1,041
AZ (nonSWB)	1,826	1,781	1,363	1,133	778	736	654	633	447	808
SUM	2,738	2,898	2,552	1,988	1,923	2,202	1,867	2,142	2,566	3,291

Figure 7.9. Heroin Seizures 2001–2010, Southwest Border and Elsewhere.

7.2.3. Comparison with Consumption Estimates

Section Four suggests that heroin consumption remained fairly stable throughout the decade, although there is some evidence of an increase in later years. Most of the heroin consumed in the United States comes from poppies grown in Colombia and Mexico, but data deficiencies surrounding associated production figures from 2005 to 2010 make comparisons difficult. There was a steady increase in the amount of heroin seized within the United States and at the southwest border from 2007 through 2010.

7.3. Methamphetamine

The meth consumed in the United States is produced both domestically and abroad. One source of foreign meth production is Southeast Asia; production from Asia that reaches the United States primarily supports consumption outside the continental United States, including Hawaii and Guam (National Drug Intelligence Center [NDIC], 2005). Mexican production is a larger concern, responsible for a substantial and growing portion of methamphetamine for mainland U.S. consumption. While we do not know the precise proportions, we do know that the share coming from Mexico has varied over time (see, e.g., Cunningham et al., 2009).

There are two major methods for producing methamphetamine, each of which uses different precursors (NDIC, 2005). The first is an ephedrine/pseudoephedrine reduction (E/P reduction), wherein ephedrine (EPH) or pseudoephedrine (PSE) are combined with various acids, alkalines, metals, and other components to produce d-methamphetamine. There are several specific formulas (called recipes) in this method, including several using iodine-based and phosphorus-based chemicals, and the Birch (or "Nazi") method, which uses anhydrous ammonia and an alkali metal such as sodium or lithium. The second major method is the Phenyl-2-propanone method (P2P), which combines the base P2P with other chemicals to produce a lower quality dlmethamphetamine.

A major constraint on methamphetamine production is the precursor chemicals. Starting with the Chemical Diversion and Trafficking Act of 1988, increased restrictions on precursor chemicals at both the state and federal level have ratcheted up the difficulty in obtaining precursor chemicals. The most recent federal law is the Combat Methamphetamine Epidemic Act of 2005 (CMEA), which expanded the limits on bulk sales of EPH and PSE, and required that EPH, PSE, and phenylpropanolamine be placed "behind the counter" with transaction logs to account for all sales. Some states take the additional step of linking those logs in a computerized database for sharing of information across locations, or requiring a prescription for precursor medications.

7.3.1. Methamphetamine Production in the United States

Methamphetamine production in the United States has historically been associated with outlaw motorcycle gangs for consumption in the western United States. To counter growing methamphetamine production, various laws restricting precursor chemicals have been implemented. The most recent of these laws on the national level was the CMEA passed in 2006. At that time, a majority of meth production by weight came from domestic super labs (O'Connor et al., 2007, p. 4). Since then, domestic production has primarily switched to small-scale laboratories, as producers had more difficulty getting precursors in larger quantities. Additionally, advances in smaller-production recipes developed in this period, making it easier for methamphetamine to be produced in spite of the quantity limitations. More recently, the number of superlabs has begun to rebound, with increased seizures of them in California beginning in 2008 (NDIC, 2010a, p. 35).

The number of methamphetamine labs seized is a commonly used indicator for methamphetamine production, although there are several challenges in interpreting seizure numbers. First, there is little evidence to support the assumption that the share of labs that are seized is stable over time. Law enforcement and criminals are engaged in a cycle of countermeasures—where law enforcement detection can improve one year, while the trafficker concealment improves the next. More importantly, the share of labs seized may be related to the size of the problem itself, where specific policy actions may lead to an increased emphasis on finding labs; paradoxically, an increase in enforcement may shut down an increased number of labs, decreasing actual production while falsely indicating an increase in production.

Second, the definition of a lab encompasses a range of variation in kinds of labs and quantities produced. The largest domestic superlabs are defined as those capable of producing 10 or more pounds in a single production cycle. DSLs typically use bulk EPH/PSE for production. STLs use over-the-counter (OTC) products containing EPH or PSE. While often STL production occurs in a house or a trailer (O'Connor et al., 2007, p.4), STLs can be very small indeed—one E/P reduction recipe called "shake and bake" produces methamphetamine in a sealed two-liter soda bottle (NDIC, 2010b, p. 35). The variation in production size can complicate national estimates of methamphetamine production based on the number of identified labs.

Despite these caveats—and the fact that these figures are voluntarily reported—the number of laboratory seizures tells a story consistent with current understandings (Figure 7.10). The number of lab seizures declined at the same time that precursor laws were coming into effect in the first half of the decade, but clearly rebounded in 2009 and 2010. Lab seizures in 2009 and 2010 were not as large as the seizures in the first half of the decade, which the DEA interprets as an increase in domestic methamphetamine production but not to the levels seen before precursor laws were strongly in place (DEA, 2012).

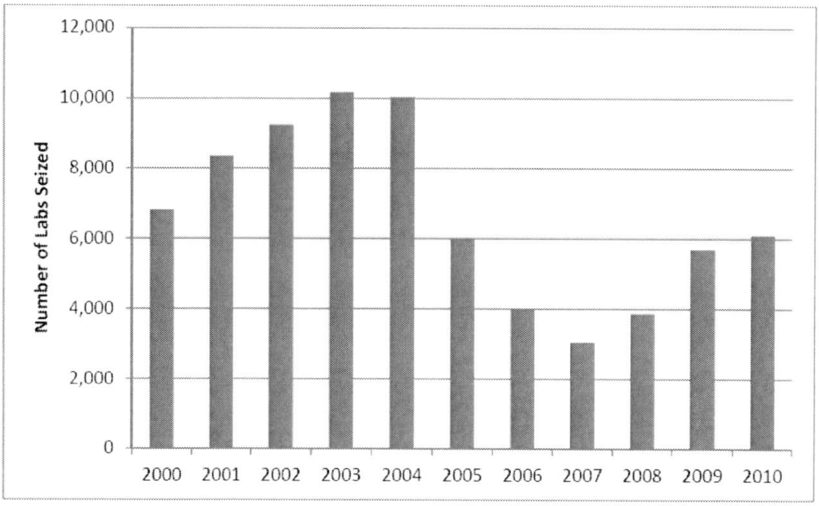

Figure 7.10. Methamphetamine Lab Seizures in the United States, 2000–2010.

7.3.2. Methamphetamine Produced or Transported through Mexico

Efforts to constrict domestic production in the United States have increased the opportunities for Mexican drug trafficking organizations (DTOs) to expand into the methamphetamine market in the United States. As a result, "Mexican [DTOs] have become the primary manufacturers and distributors of methamphetamine to cities in the Midwest and West" (DEA, 2011).

The restriction of precursor chemicals has also been undertaken in Mexico. In 2005, Mexico began to restrict the importation of precursor EPH and PSE, culminating by 2009 in a ban on both chemicals in Mexico (NDIC, 2010a, p. 34). However, DTOs in Mexico continue to obtain EPH and PSE illegally.

Due to these precursor restrictions, Mexican meth production switched to alternative production methods between 2005 and 2008. There is some evidence that methamphetamine production decreased in this period, as evidenced by the seizure of methamphetamine at the Southwest border of the United States. However, these same indicators suggest that Mexican-produced meth has rebounded and continued its increasing trend. Mexican DTOs adapted to alternative production methods by smuggling prohibited precursor chemicals, using alternative chemicals that can be used to create EPH or PSE, and using alternative production methods that do not use EPH or PSE (notably the P2P method) (NDIC, 2010a, p. 34).

With regards to the data on meth labs seized, these problems appear substantial. Data on methamphetamine laboratories seized in Mexico are available from multiple sources: the government of Mexico, as reported to the DEA and available in the National Drug Threat Assessment (NDTA) (NDIC, 2010a); and the UNODC, to which Mexico reports (Figure 7.11). A first concern is that these two present not only different counts, but also different trends. At least one of the two datasets is inaccurate. A second concern is the apparent increase in seizures. Between four times (using NDTA figures) and nine times (using UNODC figures) as many Mexican methamphetamine laboratories were reported seized in 2009 as in 2008. It seems unlikely that methamphetamine production increased by a comparable amount in those years. This concern is even more exaggerated in Mexican methamphetamine seizure data (Figure 7.10), with a nearly twentyfold increase in seizures between 2008 and 2009. The discrepancy and extremely large increases raise important questions about the validity of these series.

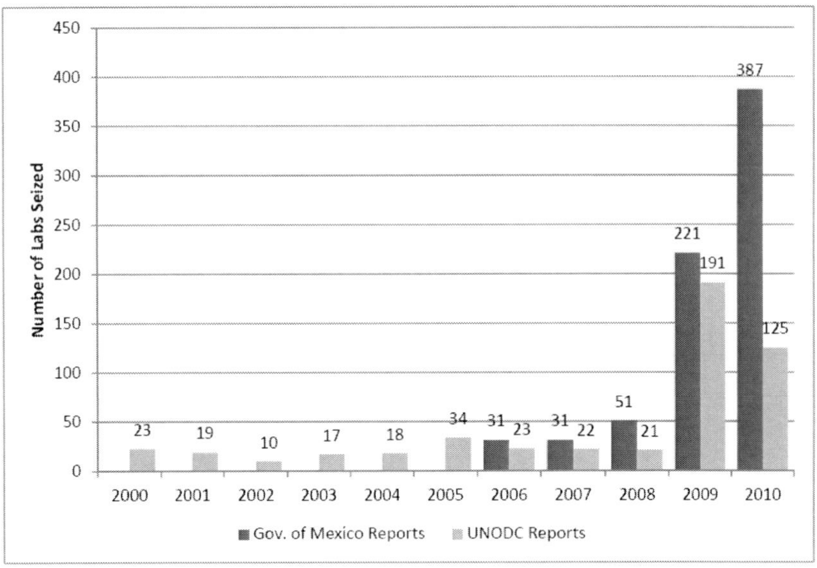

Figure 7.11. Methamphetamine Lab Seizures in Mexico, 2000–2010.

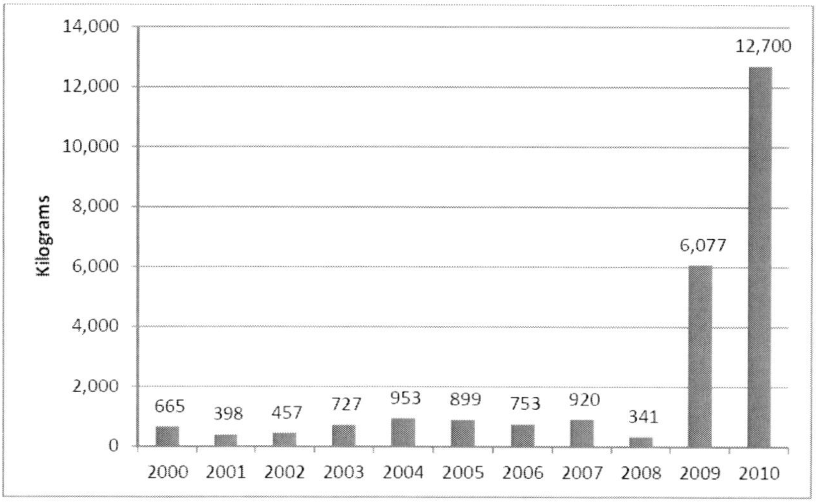

Figure 7.12. Methamphetamine Seized in Mexico, 2000–2010.

Another source of data that may inform us about Mexican methamphetamine production is the amount of methamphetamine seized at the southwest border of the United States. Figure 7.13 shows there was a decrease associated with the implementation of EPH/PSE restrictions between 2005 and 2008, but amounts have been trending upward since 2008 as DTOs adjusted.

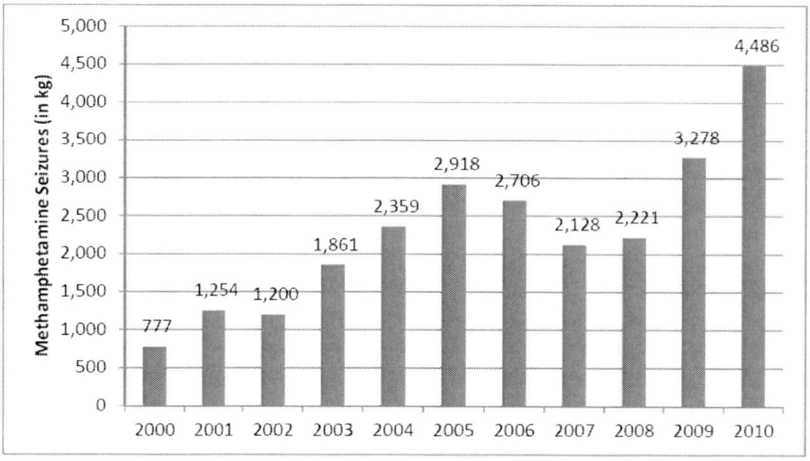

Figure 7.13. Meth Seized at the Southwest U.S. Border, 2000–2010.

Finally, if there was such a large increase in meth supply late in the decade, we would expect to see a decrease in the purity-adjusted price at the retail level in the United States. And indeed, as Figure 7.14 shows, the price per pure gram of methamphetamine tended to go down in years with large quantities seized—suggestive of abundant supply—and to go up in years when less was seized. For example, there appears to be a price decrease through 2005, an increase through 2008, and a 32- percent decline through 2010 (which continues through 2011; not displayed).

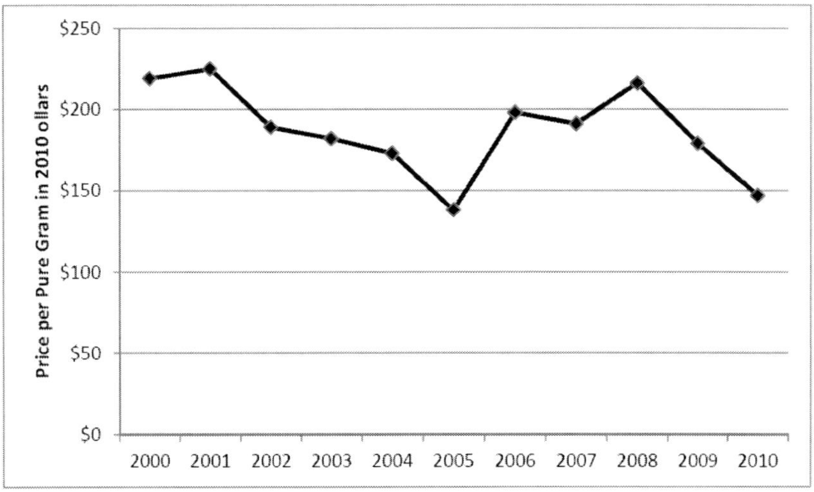

Source: ONDCP, 2013.

Figure 7.14. Price per Pure Gram of Methamphetamine, 2000–2010.

7.3.3. Comparisons with Consumption Estimates

Most of the consumption and supply-side meth indicators tell a similar story through 2008. From 2000 to 2004, there was a sharp increase in consumption; from 2004 to 2008, there was a decrease in consumption. Whether meth consumption peaked in 2004, 2005, or 2006 depends on the indicator. These trends are consistent with data about meth lab seizures in the United States, meth seized at the southwest border, and U.S. meth prices.

The similarities stop after 2008. Our consumption figures are virtually flat through 2010; QUEST positive drug tests are flat; treatment admissions decrease; emergency room visits increase; and past-month users in the household population increase in 2009, then decrease in 2010 (see Section Two). All the supply-side indicators suggest large increases from 2008 to

2010, and this is consistent with the decrease in meth prices beginning in 2009 that continue through 2011 (not displayed; ONDCP, 2013).

7.4. Marijuana

Marijuana is produced throughout the world, both outdoors and indoors. Unlike coca and opium, the yield per unit area is high enough to make it worth the effort to grow in very small batches. This makes indoor production not only a possibility, but a preferred option for those seeking to produce highly potent sinsemilla;[35] growing indoors reduces the probability that female plants are pollinated, thus increasing THC content. The geographic dispersion of production, the ability to hide outside grows, and increasing significance of indoor production all complicate efforts to generate supply-side estimates of the U.S. marijuana market.

Based on a review of national and international documents, reports from local DEA offices, and an analysis of marijuana price information from general population and arrestee surveys, Kilmer et al. (2010b) concluded that 40–67 percent of the marijuana consumed in the United States came from Mexico circa 2008. With smaller amounts of marijuana imported into the United States from Canada, Jamaica, and elsewhere, they concluded that the majority of marijuana consumed in the United States at that time was imported, with most coming from outdoor production in Mexico. Unfortunately, estimates of Mexican marijuana production have long been inconsistent and at times implausible (Reuter, 1996; Kilmer et al., 2010b).

The caveats about "circa 2008" in the previous paragraph are important. U.S. domestic production has been highly dynamic over the last decade, so the balance of domestic vs. imported marijuana has been in flux.

This section reviews the available supply-side indicators for marijuana in the United States and Mexico and compares them with the consumption estimates generated in Section Five.

7.4.1. Marijuana Production in the United States

The claim that U.S. marijuana production reaches or exceeds 10,000 MTs appears prominently in policy debates (Kilmer et al., 2011).[36] As Gettman (2007) notes, this figure appears in numerous official national and international reports, including the 2002, 2003, and 2005 INCSRs, the 2003 ***National Drug Control Strategy,*** and the United Nation's ***Global Illicit Drug Trends, 2003*** and the ***2004 World Drug Report***. However, there are no sources cited by the INCSR, the NDCS figures, or , although the U.N. reports reference the 2003 INCSR and 2003 ***National Drug Control Strategy***.

The figure may have its origins in a report published in 2002 by the Drug Availability Steering Committee (DASC),[37] which was chaired by the DEA and included representatives from other law enforcement agencies. We note the weaknesses of this estimate, but we also stress that DASC explicitly acknowledged those weaknesses.[38] For example, while DASC expressed some confidence in its cocaine estimates, with respect to U.S. marijuana production, it stated:

> The quantity of domestically produced marijuana that was available in the United States in 2001 is unknown. While the group did develop a methodology for determining such availability in the future, the uncertainty in the required data, some of which do not currently exist, is magnified by the model, and prevents the derivation of a credible estimate at this time. However, by making reasonable assumptions regarding the number of cannabis plants eradicated and the amount of marijuana potentially produced per cannabis plant, and applying a set of hypothetical values for the cannabis eradication rate, the model yields an estimate for the availability of domestic marijuana ranging between 5,577 and 16,731 metric tons (p. 103).

The DASC estimates are reproduced in Table 7.2. DASC's figure of 5,577 MTs combines plants eradicated (4,150,173) with assumptions that one marijuana plant yields about one pound (448 grams)[39] of consumable product annually, and that 25 percent of all domestically produced marijuana is seized (5,577 MTs = 4.15 million plants * 448 * (1 – 25 percent) / 25 percent). The 16,731 MTs figure is obtained by reducing the seizure rate to 10 percent. There is little agreement on the yield of a typical marijuana plant (Bouchard, 2007; Caulkins, 2010a), so DASC also displays net production figures for per plant yields of 200 grams and 1,000 grams (1 kilogram).[40]

This lack of agreement stems not just from imperfect information but also from the malleability of the marijuana plant itself. Where there is an incentive to minimize the number of plants grown (e.g., out of concern for enhanced sanctions that take effect with possession of 100 or more plants), one can grow very large plants. This is not uncommon with outdoor grows. By contrast, where the incentive is to maximize yield per unit area (e.g., when growing indoors), it is more effective to grow many small plants that are harvested more times per year. Yield also varies depending on whether only buds or also other parts of the plant are harvested. The DASC figure of one pound per plant is more representative of outdoor growing of "commercial grade" marijuana; by contrast, Toonen et al. (2006) report average yields of just 33.7 grams per plant, or a little over an ounce per plant from indoor cultivation.

Table 7.2. DASC Estimates of Domestically Produced Marijuana Potentially Available in the United States (in MTs)

Assumed Yield per Plant	Hypothetical Eradication Rate		
	10 percent	15 percent	25 percent
200 grams	7,470	4,703	2,490
448 grams (~1 pound)	16,731	10,534	5,577
1 kilo	37,350	23,516	12,450

Notes: Reproduced from DASC (2002), Table 4-2, page 109.

The DASC estimates were meant to illustrate how the calculations would work ***if*** the relevant parameters were known. Indeed, DASC explicitly states that it does not know the eradication rate: "There is currently no basis upon which to derive a credible estimate of the effectiveness of domestic cannabis eradication efforts. The figure is **unknown**" (emphasis in original; p. 116). Further highlighting the uncertainty is a memorandum at the end of the DASC report from the DEA's Statistical Services Unit with a list of alternative estimates about marijuana availability. After accounting for eradication, this memorandum states that net marijuana production in the United States was 2,355 MTs—far lower than the oft-reported 10,000 MTs and close to the lowest estimate reported in the DASC table (reproduced in Table 7.2). Even if the dubious 10,000 MTs claims trace to the DASC report, the fault for such misunderstanding does not lie with the DASC.

While it may be tempting to use seizure data to understand trends in supply, caution should be used when trying to draw inferences from seizure statistics. As noted by Reuter (1995), "the quantity seized is a function of at least three factors: (1) the quantity shipped, (2) the relative skill of the interdictors, and (3) the care taken by smugglers." Further, NSS, the most comprehensive database of seizures in the United States, does not include information from all seizures. Indeed, the DOJ's Office of the Inspector General warns that, "As a result, intelligence products based on this data (sic) may be incomplete or inaccurate."[41]

As a further complication, not all data systems distinguish the type of cannabis product seized. Sinsemilla may contain two or even three times THC per unit weight than does standard commercial-grade marijuana (Kilmer et al., 2010b). Increasingly it is standard practice to adjust cocaine and heroin estimates for variation in purity up and down the supply chain and over time, but it is not yet commonplace to attempt an analogous adjustment for THC content when tracking marijuana supply.

Some data about the eradication of marijuana plants are also collected by local, state, and federal law enforcement agencies. The DEA funds the Domestic Cannabis Eradication/Suppression Program (DCES/P) which (as of 2011) provides funding and assistance to 124 state and local law enforcement agencies to help with their cannabis eradication efforts (DEA website, undated). Figure 7.15 displays the number of indoor and outdoor plants eradicated from 1993–2010. There is a large increase in both values beginning in 2005, and this may be at least partially attributable to a shift in law enforcement priorities:

> In 2005, the Office of National Drug Control Policy (ONDCP) and DEA, along with other federal, state, and local law enforcement and intelligence agencies, identified California, Hawaii, Kentucky, Oregon, Tennessee, Washington, and West Virginia as the primary marijuana cultivation states (M7 states). After the M7 states were identified, law enforcement resources were shifted to focus eradication efforts on these states. Much of the funding used to facilitate these eradication operations is provided through DEA's DCE/SP Program. DCE/SP data show that more than 8 million plants were eradicated in 2008, 89 percent (7,136,133 plants of 8,013,308 plants) of which were eradicated in the M7 States (NDIC, 2009, 6).

Counting plants is even more problematic than counting weight seized without differentiating by type of cannabis. As noted above, yield per plant varies by more than an order of magnitude depending on the variety and nature of cultivation.

7.4.2. Marijuana Production in Mexico

While estimates of marijuana production in Mexico do exist, analysts have raised doubts about these figures (Reuter, 1996; Kilmer et al., 2010b).[42] One reason for the inconsistency in production figures over time was the lack of reliable information about typical yield. Indeed, the 2011 INCSR states that reliable information about marijuana yields were not available to estimate potential marijuana production for 2009 (U.S. State Department, 2011) and as of the 2012 INCSR, marijuana production figures were no longer generated.

As noted in Section 7.1, the U.S. government recently revised its methodological model for estimating Mexican marijuana production in 2011 and believes that the previous estimates were inflated. This raises important questions about the reliability of the previously published estimates.

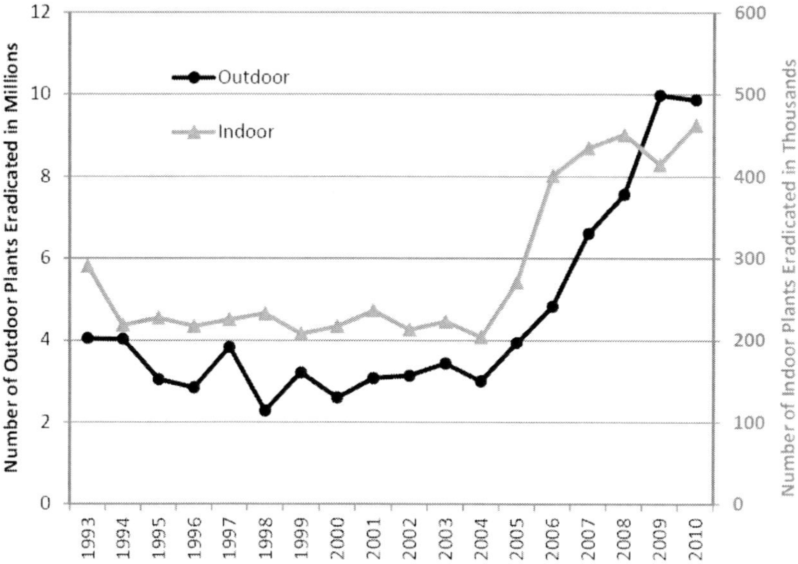

Source: DEA Domestic Cannabis Eradication and Suppression Program (DCES/P, Justice Sourcebook

Figure 7.15. Plants Eradicated as Part of the DEA's Domestic Cannabis Eradication/Suppression Program, by Year.

Now, only estimates for hectares of Mexican cultivated cannabis are reported in INCSR, and it appears there was a very large increase from 2005 to 2010 (Figure 7.16). Some attribute the increase to Mexican officials moving military and law enforcement officials away from eradication so they could address the drug-related violence plaguing the country (e.g., NDIC, 2010a).

A recent rise in cultivated hectares is consistent with the increase in seizures of marijuana at the southwest border, most of which is presumably produced in Mexico. Table 7.3 displays NSS data for kilograms of marijuana seized along the southwest border and in the rest of the United States.[43] According to the NSS, the amount of marijuana seized along the border was fairly flat from 2001 to 2006; then, from 2006 to 2010, the amount seized nearly doubled—from 1,150 MTs to 1,960 MTs.

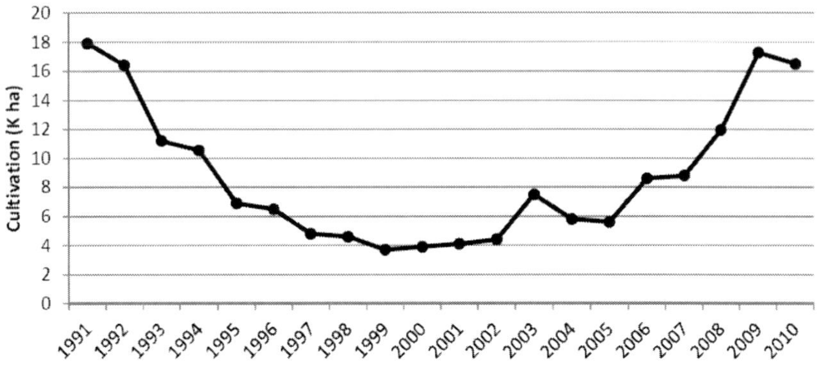

Source: International Narcotics Control Strategy Report (INCSR), State Dept, various years.

Figure 7.16. Estimates of Marijuana Cultivation in Mexico, 1991–2010.

Table 7.3. Marijuana Seized in the NSS (in MTs)

Year	United States (Non-Southwest Border)	Southwest Border	TOTAL
2001	271	1,165	1,435
2002	217	1,183	1,400
2003	303	1,345	1,648
2004	196	1,157	1,352
2005	303	1,095	1,398
2006	239	1,153	1,392
2007	288	1,475	1,763
2008	261	1,353	1,614
2009	276	1,965	2,241
2010	382	1,960	2,342

Source: NSS, as of December 1, 2012.

7.4.3. Comparison with Consumption Estimates

Our Section Five estimates suggest that marijuana consumption likely increased by approximately 40 percent from 2002 to 2010. Data from multiple sources (e.g., U.S. southwest border seizures, number of eradicated indoor grow operations, estimates of the amount of land used to cultivate marijuana in

Mexico) suggest there may have been an increase in the amounts of marijuana produced in both the United States and in Mexico after 2005. It is encouraging to see these data sources moving in the same direction, but given the limitations of the data, even that concordance is not necessarily definitive.

Seizures reported to NSS generally parallel our consumption figures. Thus, the implied seizure rate for 2002–2010 remained surprisingly stable at 25 percent and 30 percent (the gray line in Figure 7.17). That stability is noteworthy considering the series come from very different sources.

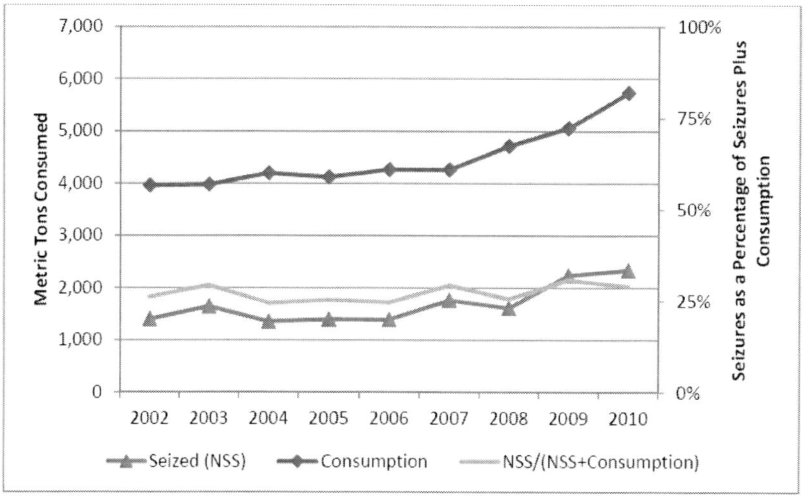

Figure 7.17. Marijuana Seizures, Consumption, Estimated Seizure Rate, 2002–2010.

7.5. Discussion

There are important challenges in comparing trends in drug consumption estimates with drug supply indicators. The error bands for most of these drug availability estimates are large; thus, caution should be used when trying to understand year-to-year changes (ONDCP, 2012b). Longer time horizons may allow for more informative comparisons.

For marijuana and cocaine, the consumption and supply-side indicators both showed similar trends suggesting large consumption changes in the last half of the decade. For 2000 to 2005, there was much less consistency. Given the large amount of uncertainty surrounding all of these figures, the pre-2005 fluctuations may be little more than noise.

With the U.S. government revising their methodology for estimating Mexican heroin production in 2011 and stating that previous estimates were inflated, it is impossible to compare these figures with our consumption estimates, which are fairly flat over the decade. Heroin seized throughout the country decreased from 2000 to 2005 and then increased through 2010, but this could be more of a reflection of enforcement priorities and smuggler precaution than consumption.

While there are also important differences in the supply- and consumption-based estimates for methamphetamine, they are not as surprising. On the demand side, national datasets do not do a good job of capturing methamphetamine use (Nicosia et al., 2009), and the absence of ADAM data during the peak of meth use in the United States makes our consumption results highly dependent on how time is incorporated into our models.

In summary, the broad trends in consumption of marijuana and cocaine appear to be reasonably well understood since they are detected in both demand and supply-side indicators. There is likewise agreement concerning an increasing trend in meth consumption over the first half of the decade and subsequent decline through 2008, but there is not comparable agreement as to the level, and we suggest that the most defensible position concerning trends in meth consumption from 2008 to 2010 is simply to admit the data are insufficient to provide clear guidance. Most of the heroin consumed in the United States comes from poppies grown in Colombia and Mexico, and data deficiencies surrounding associated production figures from 2005 to 2010 make comparisons difficult. There was a steady increase in the amount of heroin seized within the United States and at the southwest border from 2007 through 2010.

CONCLUSION

This report presents estimates of the size of the cocaine, heroin, marijuana, and methamphetamine markets in the United States for 2000 through 2010. For each substance, we estimate the total number of CDUs (defined as those using four or more times in the previous month), total weight consumed, and the total amount spent purchasing these substances. Main findings include:

- Drug users in the United States spend on the order of $100 billion annually on cocaine, heroin, marijuana, and methamphetamine. While this total figure has been stable over the decade, there have been important compositional shifts. In 2000, much more money was spent on cocaine than marijuana; in 2010 the opposite was true.
- From 2002 to 2010, the amount of marijuana consumed in the United States likely increased by about 40 percent while the amount of cocaine consumed in the United States decreased by about 50 percent. These figures are consistent with supply-side indicators, such as seizures and production estimates.
- Heroin consumption remained fairly stable throughout the decade, although there is some evidence of an increase in the later years. Most of the heroin consumed in the United States comes from poppies grown in Colombia and Mexico, but data deficiencies surrounding associated production figures from 2005 to 2010 make comparisons difficult. There was a steady increase in the amount of heroin seized within the United States and at the southwest border from 2007 through 2010.
- Methamphetamine estimates are subject to the greatest uncertainty, because national datasets do not do a good job of capturing its use (Nicosia et al., 2009). Three particular challenges were that ADAM was discontinued when methamphetamine use was believed to be at its peak (2004–2006), ADAM-II covers very few counties with substantial methamphetamine use, and NSDUH changed how it asked about methamphetamine use in 2006. While multiple indicators are consistent with an increasing trend in meth consumption over the first half of the decade and a subsequent decline through 2008, there is not comparable agreement as to the level. We suggest that the most defensible position concerning trends from 2008 to 2010 is simply to admit the data are insufficient to provide clear guidance.
- Total consumption and expenditures are driven by the minority of very heavy users who consume on 21 or more days each month.

There is great uncertainty surrounding these market size estimates, particularly for methamphetamine, and in many cases, the extent of the uncertainty cannot be bounded or quantified. Though this analysis weaves together information from a variety of indicators, survey self-reports remain a principal source of information about user behaviors—frequency, quantity, and spending. The organizations conducting these surveys expend considerable effort trying to minimize misreporting, including sometimes confirming self-reported data by testing users for the presence of drugs. Nevertheless, there is no way to entirely escape the basic limitations of survey self-report, and unfortunately supply-side estimates are plagued by different but equally severe limitations.

This raises two important questions: Can these demand-side estimates for illicit drugs be improved? And what would it take to do so?

The answer depends on the drug. In brief, we are optimistic about the possibility of refining the marijuana estimates. In contrast, we are decidedly pessimistic about meth, because much of its use falls outside the ambit of the standard data systems. The prospect of improving estimates of the size of cocaine and heroin markets largely depends on whether the surveys that reach heavy users of these two drugs could be enhanced and extended.[44]

The biggest challenges for sizing marijuana markets is obtaining information about quantity consumed per day of use and assessing the validity of self-reported surveys. The science on quantifying consumption per use day (in terms of grams and THC) is in its infancy. We know far too little about how sharing behavior is reflected in self-reports of quantity consumed and how consumption patterns vary among different categories of users. However, given the large shifts in public opinion about marijuana use (Pew, 2013), we expect this will receive more attention in the future, especially from analysts and funders interested in assessing the consequences of changing marijuana laws at the state level (see, for example, Kilmer et al., 2013). Relatively modest revisions to the questions about marijuana in NSDUH would go a long way toward resolving this challenge. For example, asking users about their past-week purchases instead of only their most recent purchase would be very helpful. With respect to assessing the validity of self-report surveys, there is an established literature, but it is relatively old and focuses more on admissions of any use (i.e., prevalence) than on quantities consumed (needed for estimating market size). Studies that validate self-reported data for a broad spectrum of users would be welcome, as would studies that assess the validity of frequency/intensity of use, not just prevalence.

The data situation for meth is dismal and unlikely to improve under the current data collection regimes. Unless serious efforts are made to systematically capture information from producers and heavy users outside of urban areas, we will remain in the dark about a relatively large segment of meth consumption.

The prospects for more accurately sizing the heroin and cocaine markets largely depend on the ability to obtain information from heavy users. These estimates have long been rooted in information from the arrestee population, but funding cuts to the ADAM program have reduced the number of participating counties from more than 40 in 2003 to ten in 2007 and just five in 2011. The well-documented geographical variation in these markets cannot be monitored when so few counties are included. The limited information about arrestee drug use after 2003 accounts for a large share of the uncertainty in our estimates. Another potential source of information about heavy users is the treatment population, but we don't know enough about how often users touch the treatment system.

Of course, there could be a technological innovation that improves our understanding of these markets. For example, the increased attention to wastewater analysis is intriguing, although its usefulness for estimating the market size for an entire country remains unproven.

The statistical models presented in Section Two demonstrate that several county-, MSA- and state-level variables are correlated with arrestee drug use. Thus, in the short run it would not be unreasonable to combine the parameters estimated from our models with more recent data on those variables to "predict" county-year averages of positive tests among arrestees (and then extrapolate to other populations). However, this cannot serve as a satisfactory long-run strategy for monitoring drug markets, as the relationships between these variables will inevitably change over time. Thus, continued investment in regular (though not necessarily annual) collection of detailed data from users, especially heavy users, is warranted.

REFERENCES

Arkes, J., Pacula, R. L., Paddock, S., Caulkins, J., & Reuter, P. (2004). *Technical report for the price and purity of illicit drugs through 2003*. Washington, D.C.: Office of National Drug Control Policy.

Arkes, J., Pacula, R.L., Paddock, S.M., Caulkins, J.P., & Reuter, P. (2008). *Why the DEA STRIDE data are still useful for understanding drug markets*. NBER Working Paper 14224.

Banta-Green, C., & Field, J. (2011). City-wide drug testing using municipal wastewater: A new tool for drug epidemiology. *Significance, 8(2)* 70–74.

Bouchard, M. (2007). A capture-recapture model to estimate the size of criminal populations and the risks of detection in marijuana cultivation industry. *Journal of Quantitative Criminology, 23,* 221–241.

Bouchard, M. (2008). Towards a realistic method to estimate the size of cannabis production in industrialized countries. *Contemporary Drug Problems*, 35, 291–320.

Bramley-Harker, E. (2001). *Sizing the UK market for illicit drugs*. Home Office RDS Occasional Paper 74, London: Home Office.

Brecht, M. Anglin, M. D. and Tzu-Hui, L. (2003). Estimating Drug Use Prevalence Among Arrestees Using ADAM Data: An Application of a Logistic Regression Synthetic Estimation Procedure. As of January 17, 2014: https://www.ncjrs.gov/pdffiles1/nij/grants

Brecht M. L., Huang D., Evans E., & Hser V. I. (2008). Polydrug use and implications for longitudinal research: Ten-year trajectories for heroin, cocaine, and methamphetamine users. *Drug and Alcohol Dependence*, *96*(3), 193–201.

Bureau of International Narcotics and Law Enforcement Affairs (Annual, 1990–2013). *International Narcotics Control Strategy Report, Drug and Chemical Control Report*. Washington, D.C.: United States Department of State.

Burgdorf, J. R., Kilmer, B., & Pacula, R. L. (2011). Heterogeneity in the composition of marijuana seized in California. *Drug and Alcohol Dependence*, *117*, 59–61.

Casey, J., Hay, G., Godfrey, C., & Parrott, S. (2009). *Assessing the scale and impact of illicit drug markets in Scotland*. Glasgow: Scottish Government Social Research.

Caulkins, J. P. (2005). *Price and purity analysis for illicit drug: Data and conceptual issues*. School of Public Policy and Management, 25.

Caulkins, J. P. (2007). Price and purity analysis for illicit drug: Data and conceptual issues. *Drug and Alcohol Dependence, 90S,* S61–S68.

Caulkins, J. P., & Baker, D. (2010). Cobweb dynamics and price dispersion in illicit drug markets. *Socio-Economic Planning Sciences*, *44*, 220–230.

Caulkins, J. P., Behrens, D. A., Knoll, C., Tragler, G., & Zuba, D. (2004). Markov chain modeling of initiation and demand: The case of the US cocaine epidemic. *Health Care Management Science, 7*(4), 319–329.

Caulkins, J. P., & Bond, B. M. (2012). Marijuana price gradients implications for exports and export-generated tax revenue for California after legalization. *Journal of Drug Issues, 42*(1), 28-45.

Caulkins, J., Everingham, S., Kilmer, B., & Midgette, G. (Forthcoming). The whole is just the sum of its parts: Limited polydrug use among the "big three" expensive drugs in the United States. *Current Drug Abuse Reviews*

Caulkins J. P., Hawken A., Kilmer B., Kleiman, M. A. R. (2012). *Marijuana legalization: What everyone needs to Know*. New York: Oxford University Press.

Caulkins, J. P., & Nicosia, N. (2010). What economics can contribute to the addiction sciences. *Addiction, 105,* 1156–1163.

Caulkins, J. P., & Pacula, R. L. (2006). Marijuana markets: Inferences from reports by the household population. *Journal of Drug Issues*, *36*(1), 173–200.

Caulkins, J. P., Pacula, R. L., Arkes, J., et al. (2004). *The price and purity of illicit drugs: 1981 through the Second Quarter of 2003*. Santa Monica: RAND Corporation on behalf of ONDCP.

Caulkins, J. P., & Padman, R. (1993). Quantity discounts and quality premia for illicit drugs. *Journal of American Statistical Association*, *88*, 748-57.

Caulkins, J., Rajderkar, S. S., & Vasudev, S. (2010). Creating price series without price data: harnessing the power of forensic data. In Kilmer, B., and Hoorens, S. (eds.). *Understanding illicit drug markets, supply reduction efforts, and drug-related crime in the European Union*. (pp. 165–197). TR755. Santa Monica, CA: RAND Corporation. As of December 12, 2013: http://www.rand.org/pubs/technical_reports/TR755.html

Chalmers, J., Bradford, D., & Jones, C. (2010). The effect of methamphetamine and heroin price on polydrug use: A behavioural economics analysis in Sydney, Australia. *International Journal of Drug Policy,* 21(5): 381–9.

Coffin, P. O., Galea, S., Ahern, J., Leon, A. C., Vlahov, D., & Tardiff, K. (2003). Opiates, cocaine and alcohol combinations in accidental drug overdose deaths in New York City, 1990–98. *Addiction*, *98*(6), 739–747.

Cook, P. J. (2008). *Paying the tab: The costs and benefits of alcohol control*. Princeton University Press.

Cunningham, J. K., Liu, L.-M., Callaghan, R. (2009). Impact of US and Canadian precursor regulation on methamphetamine purity in the United States. *Addiction, 104*: 441-453.

Darke, S., & Hall, W. (1995). Levels and correlates of polydrug use among heroin users and regular amphetamine users. *Drug and Alcohol Dependence, 39*(3), 231–5.

Dave, D. (2008). Illicit drug use among arrestees, prices and policy. *Journal of Urban Economics, 63*(2), 694–714.

DEA (2002). *Microgram Bulletin 36*(2):35. As of January 3, 2014: http://www.justice.gov/dea/pr/micrograms

DEA (2011). *Drugs of Abuse, 2011 Edition.* Washington, D.C.: Department of Justice, Drug Enforcement Agency.

Dennis, M., & Feeny, T. *GAIN Short Screener (GSS) summary guidelines for administration and scoring*. Bloomington, IL: Chestnut Health Systems; 2006.

DeSimone, J., & Farrelly, M. C. (2003). Price and enforcement effects on cocaine and marijuana demand. *Economic Inquiry, 41,* 98–115.

Drug Availability Steering Committee. (2002). *Drug availability estimates in the United States*. Washington, D.C.: U.S. Department of Justice.

Ehleringer, J.R., Casale, J.F., Barnette, J.E., Xu, X.. Lott, Mj., and Hurley, J.M.. (2011) !14C calibration curves for modern plant material from tropical regions of South American. Radiocarbon 53(4):585-594.

Ehleringer, J.R., Casale, J.F., Barnette, J.E., Xu, X.. Lott, Mj., and Hurley, J.M.. (2012) 14C analyses quantify time lag between coca leaf harvest and street-level seizure of cocaine. Forensic Science International.

European Monitoring Centre for Drugs and Drug Addiction. (2013). Statistical Bulletin. *Estimated trends in the prevalence of problem and injecting drug use, 2006–11*. As of September 15, 2013: http://www.emcdda.europa.eu /stats13#pdu:displayTables

———. (2013). *Wastewater analysis*. As of September 15, 2013: http://www.emcdda.europa.eu/wastewater

Fendrich M., Johnson, T. P., Wislar, J. S., et al. (2004). The utility of drug testing in epidemiological research: results from a general population survey. *Addiction*, *99,* 197–208.

Fries, A., Anthony, R. W. Cseko Jr., A., et al. (2008). *Technical report for the price and purity of illicit drugs: 1981–2007*. IDA Paper P-4370, Alexandria, VA: Institute for Defense Analyses.

Galbraith, J. W., Murray Kaiserman, M. (1997). Taxation, smuggling, and demand for cigarettes in Canada: Evidence from time-series data. *Journal of Health Economics*, *16,* 287–301.

Gallet, C.A. (2013) Can price get the monkey off our back? A meta-analysis of illicit drug demand. *Health Econ, 23(1)*, 55-68.

GAO(2005). *Agencies Need to Plan for Likely Declines in Drug Interdiction Assets, and Develop Better Performance Measures for Transit Zone Operations*. Document GAO-06-200. Washington, D.C.: Government Accountability Office.

Gettman, J. (2007). Lost taxes and other costs of marijuana laws. *Bulletin of Cannabis Reform, 4*. As of December 12, 2013: http://www.drugscience.org/Archive/bcr4/bcr4_index.html.

Gmel, G. & Rehm, J. (2004) Measuring alcohol consumption. *Contemporary Drug Problems*, *3*, 467- 540.

Grossman, M. (2005). *Individual behavior and substance use: The role of price*. NBER Working Paper 10948.

Hakkarainen, P., Kainulainen, H., & Perala. J. (2009). Measuring the cannabis market in Finland—A consumption-based estimate. *Contemporary Drug Problems*, *35,* 321–345.

Harrison, L. S., Martin, S. S., Enev, T., & Harrington, D. (2007). *Comparing drug testing and self-report of drug use among youths and young adults in the general population.* (SMA)07-4249. Department of Health and Human Services, Substance Abuse and Mental Health Services Administration, Office of Applied Studies, Rockville, MD.

Hamida S. B., Plute, E., Cosquer, B., Kelche, C., Jones, B. C., Cassel, J. C. (2008). Interactions between ethanol and cocaine, amphetamine, or MDMA in the rat: thermoregulatory and locomotor effects. *Psychopharmacology, 197*(1), 67–82.

Horowitz, J. L. (2001). Should the DEA's STRIDE data be used for economic analyses of markets for illegal drugs? *Journal of the American Statistical Association, 96*(456), 1254–1271.

Hunt, Dana. Arrestee Drug Abuse Monitoring Program II in the United States, 2007 [Computer file]. ICPSR25821-v2. Ann Arbor, MI: Inter-university Consortium for Political and Social Research [distributor], 2010-01-28. doi:10.3886/ICPSR25821.v2

Hunt, D., and Rhodes, W. Arrestee Drug Abuse Monitoring Program II in the United States, 2008 [Computer file]. ICPSR27221-v1. Ann Arbor, MI: Inter-university Consortium for Political and Social Research [distributor], 2010-03-31. doi:10.3886/ICPSR27221.v1

Hunt, D., and Rhodes, W. Arrestee Drug Abuse Monitoring Program II in the United States, 2009 [Computer file]. ICPSR30061-v1. Ann Arbor, MI: Inter-university Consortium for Political and Social Research [distributor], 2011-02-24. doi:10.3886/ICPSR30061.v1

Hunt, D., and Rhodes, W. Arrestee Drug Abuse Monitoring Program II in the United States, 2010 [Computer file]. ICPSR32321-v1. Ann Arbor, MI: Inter-university Consortium for Political and Social Research [distributor], 2011-11-04. doi:10.3886/ICPSR32321.v1

Inter-American Drug Abuse Control Commission [CICAD] (2010). *Mexico: Evaluation of Progress in Drug Control 2007–2009.* As of January 23 2014: http://cicad.oas.org/mem/reports/5/Full_Eval/Mexico%20-%205th %20Rd%20-%20ENG.pdf JofreBonet, M., & Petry, N. M. (2008).

Trading apples for oranges? Results of an experiment on the effects of heroin and cocaine price changes on addicts' polydrug use. *Journal of Economic Behavior & Organization*, *66,* 281–311.

Jones, C. M. (2013). Heroin use and heroin use risk behaviors among nonmedical users of prescription opioid pain relievers–United States, 2002–2004 and 2008–2010. *Drug and Alcohol Dependence, 132*(1-2), 95–100.

Jones J. D., Mogali, S., Comer S. D. (2012). Polydrug abuse: a review of opioid and benzodiazepine combination use. *Drug and Alcohol Dependence, 125*(1-2), 8–18.

Kedia, S., Sell, M. A., Relyea, G. (2007). Mono- versus polydrug abuse patterns among publicly funded clients. *Substance Abuse Treatment Prevention Policy*, *8*(2), 33.

Klee, H., Faugier, J., Hayes, C., Boulton, T., Morris, J. (1990). AIDS-related risk behaviour, polydrug use and temazepam. *British Journal of Addiction, 85,* 1125–32.

Kilmer, B., Caulkins, J. P., Pacula, R. L., Reuter, P. (2012). *The U.S. drug policy landscape: Insights and opportunities for improving the view.* OP-393-MCF. Santa Monica, CA: RAND Corporation. As of December 12, 2013: http://www.rand.org/pubs/occasional_papers/OP393.html

Kilmer, B., Caulkins, J. P., MacCoun, R., Pacula, R., & Reuter. P. H. (2010a). *Altered state? Assessing how legalization in California could influence marijuana consumption and public budgets.* OP-315. Santa Monica, CA: RAND Corporation.

Kilmer, B., J. P. Caulkins, R. MacCoun, R. Pacula, & P. H. Reuter (2010b). *Reducing Drug Trafficking Revenues and violence in Mexico: Would Legalizing Marijuana in California help?* OP-325-RC. Santa Monica: RAND Corporation. As of December 12, 2013: http://www.rand.org /pubs/occasional_papers/OP325.html

Kilmer, B., Caulkins, J., Midgette, G. Dahlkemper, L., MacCoun, R. & Pacula, R. (2013b). *Before the grand opening: Measuring Washington state's marijuana market in the last year before legalized commercial sales.* RR-466-WSLCB Santa Monica, CA: RAND Corporation.

Kilmer, B., Caulkins, J., Pacula, R. L., & Reuter, P. (2011). Bringing perspective to markets: Estimating the size of the U.S. marijuana market. *Drug and Alcohol Dependence*, *119*, 153–160.

Kilmer, B. & Pacula, R. L. (2009). *Estimating the size of the global drug market, a demand-side approach.* Report 2, Brussels: European Commission.

Kilmer B., J. Taylor, P. Hunt, & P. McGee. (2013). Sizing national heroin markets in the EU: insights from self–reported expenditures in the Czech Republic and England. In F. Trautman, B. Kilmer, & P. Turnbull (Eds.), Further Insights Into Aspects of the Illicit EU Drugs Market (pp. 257-270). Luxembourg: Publications Office of the European Union.

Lankenau, S. E., Schrager, S. M., Silva, K., Kecojevic, A., Bloom, J. J., Wong, C., Iverson, E. (2012). Misuse of prescription and illicit drugs among high-risk young adults in Los Angeles and New York. *Journal of Public Health Research, 1*(1), 22–30.

Larson, R. C., & Odoni, A. (1981). *Urban operations research*. Englewood, NJ: Prentice Hall.

Legaleye S., Lakhdar, C. B., & Spilka, S. (2008). Two ways of estimating the euro value of the illicit market for cannabis in France. *Drug and Alcohol Review*, *27*, 466–472.

Leigh, B. C., Gillmore, M. R., & Morrison, D. M. (1998). Comparison of diary and retrospective measures for recording alcohol consumption and sexual activity. *Journal of Clinical Epidemiology*, *51*(2), 119–127.

Leoncini, R., & Rentocchini, F. (under review). Let it snow! Let it snow! Let it snow! Estimating cocaine production using a novel dataset based on reported seizures of laboratories. *International Journal of Drug Policy.*

Leri F., Bruneau, J., Stewart, J. (2003). Understanding polydrug use: review of heroin and cocaine co-use. *Addiction, 98,* 7–22.

Lu, N. T., Taylor, B. G., & Riley, K. J. (2001). The validity of adult arrestee self-reports of crack cocaine use. *American Journal of Drug and Alcohol Abuse*, *27*(3), 399–419.

Matthew-Simmons F., Shanahan, M. & Ritter, A. (2011). Reported value of cannabis seizures in Australian newspapers: Are they accurate? *Drug and Alcohol Review*, *30*, 21–25.

Mariani, J. J., Brooks, D., Haney, M., & Levin, F. R. (2011). Quantification and comparison of marijuana smoking practices: blunts, joints, and pipes. *Drug and alcohol dependence*, *113*(2), 249– 251.

McCabe, S. E., Cranford, J. A., Morales, M., Young, A. (2006). Simultaneous and concurrent polydrug use of alcohol and prescription drugs: Prevalence, correlates, and consequences. *Journal of Studies on Alcohol and Drugs*, *67*(4), 529–537.

McCullagh, P., & Nelder, J. A. (1989). Generalized linear models (Monographs on statistics and applied probability 37). Chapman Hall, London.

Mehmedic, Z., Chandra, S., Slade, D., Denham, H., Foster, S., Patel, A. S., Ross, S. A., Khan, I. A., & El Sohly, M. A. (2010). Potency trends of 9-THC and other cannabinoids in confiscated cannabis preparations from 1993 to 2008. *Journal of Forensic Sciences*, *55*, 1209–1217.

Mejia D., & Posada, C. E. (2009). *Cocaine production and trafficking: What do we know?* The World Bank, Policy Research Working Paper 4618.

Merriman, D., Chaloupka, F. J., Yurekli, A. (2000). How big is the worldwide cigarette smuggling problem? In: Jha, P., Chaloupka, F. J. (eds.). *Tobacco control in developing countries*. (pp. 365–392). Oxford: Oxford University Press.

Mohamed, W. M., Ben Hamida, S., Cassel, J. C., de Vasconcelos, A. P., Jones, B. C.. (2011). MDMA: interactions with other psychoactive drugs. *Pharmacology Biochemistry and Behavior, 99*(4), 759– 774.

Mohler-Kuo, M., Lee, J. E., & Wechsler, H. (2003). Trends in marijuana and other illicit drug use among college students: results from 4 Harvard School of Public Health college alcohol study surveys: 1993–2001. *Journal of American College of Health*, *52*(1), 17–24.

Moore, S. C. (2010). Substitution and complementarity in the face of alcohol-specific policy interventions. *Alcohol and Alcoholism*, *45*(5), 403–408.

National Drug Intelligence Center. (2005). *Methamphetamine drug threat assessment*. As of December 12, 2013: http://www.justice.gov /archive/ndic/pubs13/13853/product.htm#Top

———. (2010a) *National drug threat assessment: 2010*. Product No. 2010-Q0317-001. U.S. Department of Justice. As of December 12, 2013: http://www.justice.gov/archive/ndic/pubs38/38661/38661p.pdf

———. (2010b) *Philadelphia/Camden High Intensity Drug Trafficking Area Drug Market Analysis 2010*. Product No. 2010-R0813-027. U.S. Department of Justice. As of January 22, 2014: http://www.justice.gov/archive/ndic/pubs40/40398/product.htm

NDIC—*See* National Drug Intelligence Center.

Nelson, D. E., Naimi, T. S., Brewer, R. D., & Roeber, J. (2010) US state alcohol sales compared to survey data, 1993-2006. *Addiction, 105*(9), 1589-1596

Nicosia, N. Pacula, R. L., Kilmer, B., Lundberg, R., & Chiesa, J. (2009). *The Economic Cost of Methamphamine Use in the Unitied States, 2005*. Santa Monica, CA: RAND Corporation. As of December 30, 2013: http://www.rand.org/pubs/monographs/MG829.html

O'Connor, J., Chriqui, J., McBride, D., Eidson, S. S., Baker, C., Terry-McElrath, Y., & vanderWaal, C. (2007). *A Report on state methamphetamine laws and regulations, effective October 1, 2005.* Washington, D. C.: National Institute of Justice.

ONDCP—*See* Office of National Drug Control Policy.

Office of National Drug Control Policy. (1991). *What America's users spend on illegal drugs*. Washington, D.C.: Executive Office of the President.

Office of National Drug Control Policy. (2001). *What America's users spend on illegal drugs*. Washington, D.C.: Executive Office of the President.

Office of National Drug Control Policy. (2008). *Cocaine smuggling in year 2007*. Washington, D.C.: Executive Office of the President.

Office of National Drug Control Policy. (2010). *Cocaine smuggling in year 2008*. Washington, D.C.: Executive Office of the President.

Office of National Drug Control Policy. (2011). *Cocaine smuggling in year 2009*. Washington, D.C.: Executive Office of the President.

Office of National Drug Control Policy. (2012a). *Cocaine smuggling in year 2010*. Washington, D.C.: Executive Office of the President.

Office of National Drug Control Policy. (2012b). *Drug availability estimates in the United States: 2000-2006*. Washington, D.C.: Executive Office of the President.

Office of National Drug Control Policy. (2012c). *What America's users spend on illegal drugs, 2000– 2006*. Washington, D.C.: Executive Office of the President.

Office of National Drug Control Policy (2013). *National drug control strategy: 2013 data supplement*. Washington, D.C.: Executive Office of the President.

Pacula, R. L., Grossman, M., Chaloupka, F. J., O'Malley, P., et al. (2001). Marijuana and youth. In: J. Gruber (Ed.) *Risky behavior among youths: An economic analysis*. Chicago, IL: University of Chicago Press.

Pacula, R. L., Kilmer, B., Grossman, M., & Chaloupka, F. J. (2010). Risks and prices: The role of user sanctions in marijuana markets. *The BE Journal of Economic Analysis & Policy, 10*(1), 1–36.

Paoli, L., Greenfield, V., Reuter, P. (2009). *The world heroin market: Can supply be cut?* Oxford University Press.

Pew Center for the People & the Press (2013). *Majority Now Supports Legalizing Marijuana*.

Washington, DC: Pew Research Center. As of January 13, 2014: http://www.people-press.org/2013/04/04/majority

Pudney, S. E., Badillo, C., Bryan, M., Burton, J., Conti, G., & Iacovou, M. (2006). Estimating the size of the UK illicit drugs market, in *Measuring different aspects of problem drug use: Methodological developments, home office online report 16/06*, London: Home Office 46–120.

Reuter, P., 1995. Seizure of drugs. In: Encyclopedia of Drugs and Alcohol. MacMillan, New York

Reuter, P. (1996). The Mismeasurement of Illegal Drug Markets: The Implications of Its Irrelevance in Pozo, S. (ed.) *The Underground Economy.* Kalamazoo, Mich: W.E. Upjohn Institute for Employment Research, pp.63-80.

Reuter, P., & Greenfield, V. (2001). Measuring global drug markets: How good are the numbers and why should we care about them? *World Economics*, *2*(4), 159–173.

Rhodes, W., Johnston, P., Han, S., McMullen, Q., & Hozik, L. (2002). *Illicit drugs: Price elasticity of demand and supply.* Cambridge, MA: Abt Associates.

Rhodes, W., Langenbahn, S., Kling, R., & Scheiman, P. (1997). *What America's user spend on illicit drugs*. Cambridge, MA: Abt Associates.

Rhodes, W., Kling, R., & Johnston, P. (2007). Using booking data to model drug user arrest rates: a preliminary to estimating the prevalence of chronic drug use. *Journal of Quantitative Criminology*, *23*(1), 1–22.

Schulz S. (2011). MDMA & cannabis: a mini-review of cognitive, behavioral, and neurobiological effects of co-consumption. *Current Drug Abuse Review* *4*(2), 81–86.

Shelley, D., Cantrell, D. M., Moon-Howard, J., et al. (2007). The $5 man: The underground economic response to a large cigarette tax increase in New York City, *American Journal of Public Health* *97*(8), 1483–1488.

Smith, G. W., Farrell, M., Bunting, B. P., Houston, J. E., Shevlin, M. (2011). Patterns of polydrug use in Great Britain: Findings from a national household population survey. *Drug and Alcohol Dependence, 15*(113), 222–228.

Stavridis, J. G. (2010). *Partnership for the Americas,* Washington, D.C: National Defense University, November 2010. As of January 22, 2014: http://www.ndu.edu/press/lib/pdf/books/stavridis.pdf

Steentoft, A., Teige, B., Holmgren, P., Vuori, E., Kristinsson, J., Hansen, A. C., Ceder, G., Wethe, G., Rollmann, D. (2006). Fatal poisoning in Nordic drug addicts in 2002. *Forensic Science International, 160*(2-3), 148–156.

Substance Abuse and Mental Health Services Administration. 2012. *Drug abuse warning network, 2010: Area profiles of drug-related mortality.* HHS Publication No. (SMA) 12-4699, DAWN Series D-36 Rockville, MD: Substance Abuse and Mental Health Services Administration.

Thoumi, F. E. (2005). The numbers game: Let's all guess the size of the illegal drug industry! *Journal of Drug Issues*, *35*(1), 185–200.

Toonen, M., Ribot, S., and Thissen, J. (2006). Yield of illicit indoor cannabis cultivation in the Netherlands. *J Forensic Sci 51*(5): 1050-4.

UNODC—*See* United Nations Office on Drugs and Crime.

United Nations Office on Drugs and Crime (2005). *World Drug Report 2005*. UNODC, Vienna. United Nations Office on Drugs and Crime (2008). *2008 Global ATS Assessment*. UNODC, Vienna. United Nations Office on Drugs and Crime (2009). *World Drug Report 2009*. UNODC, Vienna. United Nations Office on Drugs and Crime (2010). *World Drug Report 2010*. UNODC, Vienna. United Nations Office on Drugs and Crime (2011). *World Drug Report 2011*. UNODC, Vienna.

U.S. Department of Justice. (2010). *Review of the Drug Enforcement Administration's El Paso Intelligence Center*. U.S. Department of Justice, Office of the Inspector General, Evaluation and Inspections Division. As of December 12, 2013: http://www.justice.gov/oig/reports/DEA

United States Department of Health and Human Services. Substance Abuse and Mental Health Services Administration. Office of Applied Studies. National Household Survey on Drug Abuse, 2000 [Computer file]. ICPSR03262-v4. Ann Arbor, MI: Inter-university Consortium for Political and Social Research [distributor], 2006-12-07. doi:10.3886 /ICPSR03262.v4

United States Department of Health and Human Services. Substance Abuse and Mental Health Services Administration. Office of Applied Studies. National Household Survey on Drug Abuse, 2001 [Computer file]. ICPSR03580-v3. Ann Arbor, MI: Inter-university Consortium for Political and Social Research [distributor], 2006-12-07. doi:10.3886 /ICPSR 03580.v3

United States Department of Health and Human Services. Substance Abuse and Mental Health Services Administration. Office of Applied Studies. National Survey on Drug Use and Health, 2002 [Computer file]. ICPSR03903-v3. Ann Arbor, MI: Inter-university Consortium for Political and Social Research [distributor], 2006-10-26. doi:10.3886 /ICPSR 03903.v3

United States Department of Health and Human Services. Substance Abuse and Mental Health Services Administration. Office of Applied Studies. National Survey on Drug Use and Health, 2003 [Computer file]. ICPSR04138-v2. Ann Arbor, MI: Inter-university Consortium for Political and Social Research [distributor], 2006-10-17. doi:10.3886/ICPSR04138.v2

United States Department of Health and Human Services. Substance Abuse and Mental Health Services Administration. Office of Applied Studies. National Survey on Drug Use and Health, 2004 [Computer file]. ICPSR04373-v1. Ann Arbor, MI: Inter-university Consortium for Political and Social Research [distributor], 2006-05-12. doi:10.3886/ICPSR04373.v1

United States Department of Health and Human Services. Substance Abuse and Mental Health Services Administration. Office of Applied Studies. National Survey on Drug Use and Health, 2005 [Computer file]. ICPSR04596-v2. Ann Arbor, MI: Inter-university Consortium for Political and Social Research [distributor], 2009-08-12. doi:10.3886/ICPSR04596.v2

United States Department of Health and Human Services. Substance Abuse and Mental Health Services Administration. Office of Applied Studies. National Survey on Drug Use and Health, 2006 [Computer file]. ICPSR21240-v4. Ann Arbor, MI: Inter-university Consortium for Political and Social Research [distributor], 2009-08-12. doi:10.3886/ICPSR21240.v4

United States Department of Health and Human Services. Substance Abuse and Mental Health Services Administration. Office of Applied Bibliographic Citation: Studies. National Survey on Drug Use and Health, 2007 [Computer file]. ICPSR23782-v2. Ann Arbor, MI: Inter-university Consortium for Political and Social Research [distributor], 2009-08-12. doi:10.3886/ICPSR23782.v2

United States Department of Health and Human Services. Substance Abuse and Mental Health Services Administration. Office of Applied Studies. National Survey on Drug Use and Health, 2008 [Computer file]. ICPSR26701-v2. Ann Arbor, MI: Inter-university Consortium for Political and Social Research [distributor], 2009-12-16. doi:10.3886/ICPSR26701.v2

United States Department of Health and Human Services. Substance Abuse and Mental Health Services Administration. Office of Applied Studies. National Survey on Drug Use and Health, 2009 [Computer file]. ICPSR29621-v1. Ann Arbor, MI: Inter-university Consortium for Political and Social Research [distributor], 2010-11-16. doi:10.3886/ICPSR29621.v1

United States Department of Health and Human Services. Substance Abuse and Mental Health Services Administration. Center for Behavioral Health Statistics and Quality. National Survey on Drug Use and Health, 2010 [Computer file]. ICPSR32722-v1. Ann Arbor, MI: Inter-university Consortium for Political and Social Research [distributor], 2011-12-05. doi:10.3886/ICPSR32722.v1

U.S. Dept. of Justice, National Institute of Justice. ARRESTEE DRUG ABUSE MONITORING (ADAM) PROGRAM IN THE UNITED STATES, 2000 [Computer file]. ICPSR version. Washington, DC: U.S. Dept. of Justice, National Institute of Justice [producer], 2001. Ann Arbor, MI: Inter-university Consortium for Political and Social Research [distributor], 2001. doi:10.3886/ICPSR03270.v1

United States Department of Justice. National Institute of Justice. ARRESTEE DRUG ABUSE MONITORING (ADAM) PROGRAM IN THE UNITED STATES, 2001 [Computer file]. ICPSR version. Washington, DC: United States Department of Justice. National Institute of Justice [producer], 2003. Ann Arbor, MI: Inter-university Consortium for Political and Social Research [distributor], 2003. doi:10.3886/ICPSR03688.v1

U.S. Dept. of Justice, National Institute of Justice. ARRESTEE DRUG ABUSE MONITORING (ADAM) PROGRAM IN THE UNITED STATES, 2002 [Computer file]. ICPSR version. Washington, DC: U.S. Dept. of Justice, National Institute of Justice [producer], 2003. Ann Arbor, MI: Inter-university Consortium for Political and Social Research [distributor], 2004. doi:10.3886/ICPSR03815.v1

U.S. Dept. of Justice, National Institute of Justice. ARRESTEE DRUG ABUSE MONITORING (ADAM) PROGRAM IN THE UNITED STATES, 2003 [Computer file]. ICPSR version. Washington, DC: U.S. Dept. of Justice, National Institute of Justice [producer], 2004. Ann Arbor, MI: Inter-university Consortium for Political and Social Research [distributor], 2004. doi:10.3886/ICPSR04020.v1

U.S. Drug Enforcement Administration. (2003). Microgram Bulletin (Vol. XXXVI, No. 2). As of September 15, 2013: http://www.cognitive liberty

———. (2012) *FY 2012 performance budget congressional submission*. U.S. Department of Justice. As of December 12, 2013: http://www.justice.gov/jmd/2012justification/pdf/fy12-dea-justification

———. (Undated). *Cannabis Eradication*. As of December 9, 2013: http://www.justice.gov/dea/ops/cannabis

van Laar, M., Frijns, T., Trautmann, F., & Lombi, L. (2013). Cannabis market: user types, availability and consumption estimates. In Trautman, F.,

Kilmer, B., and Turnbull, P. (eds.). *Further insights into aspects of the illicit EU drugs market*. (pp. 73_182). Luxembourg: Publications Office of the European Union.

van Nuijs, A. L., Castiglioni, S., Tarcomnicu, I., Postigo, C., de Alda, M. L., Neels, H.,Zuccato, E., Barcelo, D., & Covaci, A. (2011). Illicit drug consumption estimations derived from wastewater analysis: a critical review. *Science of the Total Environment*, *409*(19), 3564–3577.

Vopravil, J., & Běláčková, V. (2012). Illicit drug market and its economic impact. In Vopravil, J. & Rossi, C. *Illicit drug market and its economic impact*. Rome: UniversItalia.

Wilkins, C., Reilly, J., Pledger, M., & Casswell, S. (2005). Estimating the dollar value of the illicit market for cannabis in New Zealand. *Drug and Alcohol Review*, *24,* 1–8.

Wilkins, C., & Sweetsur, P. (2007). Individual dollar expenditure and earnings from cannabis in the New Zealand population. *International Journal of Drug Policy*, *18,* 187–193.

Williams, R. J., & Nowatzki, N. (2005). Validity of adolescent self-report of substance use. *Substance Use and Misuse, 40*(3), 299–311.

Williams, J., Pacula, R. L.,Chaloupka, F. J., & Wechsler, H. (2004). Alcohol and marijuana use among college students: Economic complements or substitutes? *Health Economics*, *13*, 825–843.

Williams, J., Pacula, R. L., Chaloupka, F. J., & Wechsler, H. (2006). College students' use of cocaine. *Substance Use & Misuse*, *41,* 489–509.

Xu, J. Q., Kochanek, K. D., Murphy, S. L., & Tejada-Vera, B. (2010). *Deaths: final data for 2007.* Hyattsville, MD: U.S. Department of Health and Human Services, CDC, National Center for Health Statistics. National Vital Statistics Reports 20; 58(19). As of December 12, 2013: http://www.cdc.gov/nchs/data/nvsr/nvsr58/nvsr58_19.pdf

End Notes

[1] The accompanying Technical Report includes an annotated bibliography of many of the studies published since 2000.

[2] Unless otherwise specified, cocaine should be understood to mean cocaine in all forms, including crack.

[3] This section closely follows Kilmer, Caulkins, Pacula, & Reuter (2011).

[4] There is another demand-side approach that uses wastewater analysis to measure drug consumption in an area. We do not consider this emerging method in this report. For more

information, see Banta-Green and Field (2011), van Nuijs et al. (2011), and European Monitoring Centre for Drugs and Drug Addiction (2013b).

[5] We are unaware of reliable production estimates for synthetic drugs.

[6] Gmel and Rehm (2004) on estimating alcohol consumption: "Survey-based estimates usually cover only 30%– 70% of per capita consumption derived from aggregate estimates such as sales statistics (e.g., Knibbe and Bloomfield, 2001; Rehm, 1998b). This has commonly been interpreted to mean that survey estimates are underestimates of true consumption (Alanko, 1984; Midanik, 1982). Sometimes coverage rates may be higher—e.g., in the European Comparative Alcohol Study (Leifman et al., 2002), where coverage rates of over 90% were found for the U.K. Recently, for New Zealand, high coverage rates were reported (Casswell et al., 2002). Another example is the survey by the Mexican Institute of Psychiatry, which was analyzed for the comparative risk analyses of the Global Burden of Disease Study. The volume of drinking calculated on the basis of this survey provided a higher per capita estimate for Mexico compared with a per capita estimate from sales and production data plus the estimate of unrecorded consumption (Rehm et al., in press). Coverage rates are generally high in Mexico, at around 85%–95% (Caetano, 2001). However, survey estimates that are close to or higher than estimates from sales and production statistics are still the exception rather than the rule. For most surveys, a coverage of 40%–60% can be assumed (Caetano, 2001)."

[7] Section Six addresses polydrug use and finds there is only modest overlap among demand for these three drugs. In particular, the number of chronic users of these substances in total is only about 10 percent below a naïve estimate obtained by simply summing the numbers of chronic users for each of the three substances while ignoring polydrug use entirely.

[8] Roughly consistent with Pacula, Kilmer, Grossman, & Chaloupka (2010), we do not consider arrest data from counties with coverage indicators below 65. The coverage indicator is an indicator of the quality of the data made available to the FBI and ranges from 0 (no information) to 100 (complete information). Imputations are made for counties with coverage indicators less than 100.

[9] We do not attempt to explain why there was such a large increase in cocaine overdose deaths from 2000 to 2006 given the stability in CDUs, but hope this receives more attention.

[10] One may be concerned that our estimates are inflated by the increased prevalence of prescription opiates, but great care was taken to make sure the analysis specifically focused on heroin.

[11] This is not driven by an increase in methadone treatment admissions for prescription opioid abuse; almost identical post-2007 results are obtained if the N-SSATS variable is dropped from the prediction model.

[12] The accompanying NSDUH report does not offer an explanation; it only mentions that heroin initiations did not change significantly between 2005 and 2007.

[13] We did not use this mortality variable in our prediction model because we were worried about picking up a possible increase in other psychostimulants, including other amphetamines.

[14] Multiplying by 1.125 implies bartering accounts for 11 percent of acquisitions.

[15] Basing price series for referent purchases on STRIDE makes the strong implicit assumption that prices in the market generally are comparable to those made by enforcement agents and/or their confidential informants, an assumption that is all but unavoidable in an exercise of this sort, but which has been challenged in the literature (Horowitz, 2001).

[16] The NSDUH prompts users in this part of the survey with the statement, "Sometimes people take some tobacco out of a cigar and replace it with marijuana. This is sometimes called a "blunt."

[17] Kilmer et al. (2013) concluded that a plausible aggregate adjustment could range from 1.02 to 1.43 for Washington state in 2013; however, they note that arguments can be made for values that are lower or higher. Since there are reasons to believe that underreporting may be less of an issue in Washington than in the rest of the country, these values could be too low for the nation as a whole. But since we are already making separate adjustments for youth and arrestees, our adjustment factor for adults who have not been arrested should be lower than it would be if we were trying to come up with one factor for the country. Thus, for NSDUH population adjustment we use 1.25, which is close to the middle value for Kilmer et al. (forthcoming) and other national NSDUH adjustments (Kilmer et al., 2011; ONDCP, 2012c).

[18] Estimates discussed in this Section include infrequent nonchronic users, differing from the estimates of chronic users shown in Table S2.

[19] Much of this Section's material is also presented in a paper forthcoming in *Current Drug Abuse Reviews* (Caulkins, Everingham, Kilmer, & Midgette, 2013)

[20] There are separate questions concerning past-month use days of crack and powder cocaine. Answers to the two questions were summed, but the sum was capped at 30. Since both forms can be consumed on the same day, this may inflate the number of days of cocaine use, but that bias is conservative with respect to the overall conclusion of modest polydrug use.

[21] Caulkins et al. (2013) report parallel statistics for just male defendants; the results are very similar .

[22] We find that the greatest polydrug use is among daily/near-daily heroin users, who often also use cocaine.

[23] This Section benefited from discussions with representatives from various law enforcement and military officials. All remaining errors should only be attributed to the authors.

[24] To be more precise, we took the product within each category of users (defined by past-month frequency) and then summed over categories; that accounts for the positive association between frequency and intensity of use in a way that literally multiplying average use days by average quantity used per day of use would not.

[25] Seizures of a pound or less—even though there are many of them—account for a minority of the total weight seized. Only 6 percent of the roughly 1.5 million drug arrests each year are for cocaine or heroin sale/manufacture (FBI, 2012, Table 29). Even if every single one involved a pound of cocaine, that would still only be 40 MTs.

[26] Another possibility is drawing down of excess capacity built up in other years. A tacit assumption in efforts to reconcile production and consumption figures in any given year is that changes in inventory are not large, an assumption that is hard to validate.

[27] NSDUH's unclassified table 7B reports "2.4 percent prevalence rate from 2011WDR, according to SAMHSA." Table 6.1.1.2 of the 2011 WDR reports this figure was from the 2009 Household Survey and reported by SAMHSA. Other assumptions are from the 2010 IACM (Text Box, p. 94). For HCI consumers in the United States: "40 percent of users are heavy users and consumed every 3 out of 4 days (274), and 60 percent of users are moderate and consume every 3 out of 4 weeks (39), and recreational users consume 5 grams per year." For crack consumers in the United States: "50 percent of users are heavy users and consume every day (365), and 50 percent of users are moderate and consume every week (52), and recreational users consume 9 grams per year." Heavy and moderate users reported using in past-month, recreational users are those who used in the past year but not the past month. Although not explicitly stated, it appears as if the values in parentheses represent use

days and annual grams consumed (i.e., 1 gram per use day). Sources for these assumptions were not documented for the United States or other countries.

[28] The UNODC series for U.S. cocaine consumption (WDR 2011, Table 87) is based on an extrapolation of the 2000 estimates produced by Abt (2001) for ONDCP. As this methodology has now been updated twice since those results were published (once by the same set of authors), we are cautious about giving these estimates too much weight; however, for 2006–2009 they show a 37-percent reduction in cocaine consumption with the estimate for 2009 being 157 MTs, with a range of 133 to 211 MTs.

[29] For a description of DMP, see DEA DMP (November 2008).

[30] See for example, U.S. Department of Justice and NDIC (2011).

[31] This paragraph was based on personal communication with Michael Cala of ONDCP in July 2013.

[32] In Figure 7.6, the classification is "SOAM" (South America). Estimates of opium poppy production in South American countries other than Colombia are negligible.

[33] For a discussion of the availability of data on heroin consumption for Colombia, see Paoli, Greenfield and Reuter, 2010 (Chapter 8).

[34] For example, the only treatment data available by drug of abuse of clients is for *Youth Integration Services*. These are not described in the report, but if this covers only younger drug users, it will not include a large share of heroin-dependent population, which is characteristically over age 25.

[35] "Sin semilla" means "without seed" in Spanish and is a term used figuratively for unfertilized female cannabis plants.

[36] Parts of this section were previously published in Kilmer et al. (2011).

[37] Since the 2002 INCSR report was published in 2003, it could have been influenced by the DASC report.

[38] Indeed, the DASC (2002) report is an exemplar of sensible analysis that was sensitive to its own limitations; the world of drug policy would be better informed if all government reports matched its integrity in this regard. Our criticism is not with the original authors, but rather with the subsequent repeated acceptance of the figure without acknowledgement of its limitations.

[39] It is unclear why this figure listed in the text; there are 454 grams in one pound.

[40] DASC observes about yield estimates: "There is no single agreed upon estimate for the average quantity of marijuana that can be produced from a single cannabis plant. The Royal Canadian Mounted Police uses an estimate of 170 to 200 grams per plant in estimating marijuana production in Canada. DEA uses an estimate of approximately 1 pound (448 grams) per plant based on a University of Mississippi study published in June 1992 and the USFS uses an estimate of 1 kilogram."

[41] From U.S. Department of Justice and NDIC (2010): "First, EPIC has not developed the National Seizure System into a comprehensive database into which all drug seizures are reported nationwide. Rather, reporting seizure information into the system is optional for most federal, state, and local agencies. As a result, intelligence products based on this data may be incomplete or inaccurate."

[42] Reuter (1996) documented the "fundamental unsoundness" of the estimates from the late 1980s. Notably, the 1990 INCSR Report (Bureau of International Narcotics and Law Enforcement Affairs, 1990) showed an increase in Mexican marijuana production from 5,700 MTs in 1988 to 47,000 MTs in 1989 because of "changes in estimation techniques," without explaining what the changes were. Likewise, no explanation was given for why the 1994 INCSR later reduced the 1989 figure from 47,000 MTs to a still-high 30,200 MTs.

After another aberrant year (19,700 MTs in 1990), the estimates returned to more plausible values, beginning with 7,775 MTs in 1991 (Bureau of International Narcotics and Law Enforcement Affairs, 1994). For Mexican production estimates, the figures remained between 5,300 and 11,300 MTs for 15 years before rising sharply in the early 2000s, again without a convincing explanation. While INCSR's supply-side estimates suggest that net production in Mexico almost tripled between 2001 and 2008 (from 7,400 MTs to 21,500 MTs), we demonstrate in Section Five that marijuana consumption remained quite stable during that period.

[43] Since U.S. Customs and Border Protection (CBP) makes a large share of seizures on the southwest border and they are a federal agency, the aforementioned concern about missing NSS information may be less of a concern in this context.

[44] The market for diverted pharmaceuticals fell outside the scope of this report, but its estimation may also require investments in additional primary data collection.

In: Illegal Drugs in the U.S.
Editor: Lesley Harper
ISBN: 978-1-63117-972-3
© 2014 Nova Science Publishers, Inc.

Chapter 2

DRUGS OF ABUSE [HEROIN, COCAINE, METHAMPHETAMINE, AND MARIJUANA][*]

Drug Enforcement Agency

HEROIN

What Is Heroin?

Heroin is a highly addictive drug and the most rapidly acting of the opiates.

What Is Its Origin?

Heroin is processed from morphine, a naturally occurring substance extracted from the seed pod of certain varieties of poppy plants grown in:

- Southeast Asia (Thailand, Laos, and Myanmar (Burma)),
- Southwest Asia (Afghanistan and Pakistan),
- Mexico, and Colombia

---

[*] This is an edited, reformatted and augmented version of select material from Drugs of Abuse, 2011 Edition, A DEA Resource Guide.

It comes in several forms, the main one being "black tar" from Mexico (found primarily in the western United States) and white heroin from Colombia (primarily sold on the East Coast).

What Are Common Street Names?

Common street names for heroin include:

- Big H,
- Black Tar,
- Chiva,
- Hell Dust,
- Horse, Negra,
- Smack,
- and Thunder

What Does It Look Like?

Heroin is typically sold as a white or brownish powder, or as the black sticky substance known on the streets as "black tar heroin." Although purer heroin is becoming more common, most street heroin is "cut" with other drugs or with substances such as sugar, starch, powdered milk, or quinine.

How Is It Abused?

Heroin can be injected, smoked, or sniffed/snorted. High purity heroin is usually snorted or smoked.

What Is Its Effect on the Mind?

Because it enters the brain so rapidly, heroin is particularly addictive, both psychologically and physically. Heroin abusers report feeling a surge of euphoria or "rush," followed by a twilight state of sleep and wakefulness.

What Is Its Effect on the Body?

One of the most significant effects of heroin use is addiction. With regular heroin use, tolerance to the drug develops. Once this happens, the abuser must use more heroin to achieve the same intensity. As higher doses of the drug are used over time, physical dependence and addiction to the drug develop.

Physical symptoms of heroin use include:

- Drowsiness,
- respiratory depression,
- constricted pupils,
- nausea,
- a warm flushing of the skin,
- dry mouth, and heavy extremities

What Are Its Overdose Effects?

Because heroin abusers do not know the actual strength of the drug or its true contents, they are at a high risk of overdose or death.

The effects of a heroin overdose are:

- Slow and shallow breathing,
- blue lips and fingernails,
- clammy skin,
- convulsions,
- coma, and possible death

Which Drugs Cause Similar Effects?

Other opioids such as OxyContin®, Vicodin®, codeine, morphine, methadone, and fentanyl can cause similar effects as heroin.

What Is Its Legal Status in the United States?

Heroin is a Schedule I substance under the Controlled Substances Act meaning that it has a high potential for abuse, no currently accepted medical use in treatment in the United States, and a lack of accepted safety for use under medical supervision.

COCAINE

What Is Cocaine?

Cocaine is an intense, euphoria-producing stimulant drug with strong addictive potential.

What Is Its Origin?

Cocaine is derived from coca leaves grown in Bolivia, Peru, and Colombia. The cocaine manufacturing process takes place in remote jungle labs where the raw product undergoes a series of chemical transformations. Colombia produces about 90% of the cocaine powder reaching the United States. According to the 2005 Colombia Threat Assessment, 90% of the cocaine shipped to the United States comes from the Central America-Mexico corridor.

What Are Common Street Names?

Common street names include:

- Coca,
- Coke,
- Crack,
- Flake,
- Snow,
- and Soda Cot

What Does It Look Like?

Cocaine is usually distributed as a white, crystalline powder. Cocaine is often diluted ("cut") with a variety of substances, the most common of which are sugars and local anesthetics.

It is "cut" to stretch the amount of the product and increase profits for dealers. In contrast, cocaine base (crack) looks like small, irregularly shaped chunks (or "rocks") of a whitish solid.

How Is It Abused?

Powdered cocaine can be snorted or injected into the veins after dissolving in water. Cocaine base (crack) is smoked, either alone or on marijuana or tobacco. Cocaine is also abused in combination with an opiate, like heroin, a practice known as "speedballing."

Although injecting into veins or muscles, snorting, and smoking are the common ways of using cocaine, all mucous membranes readily absorb cocaine. Cocaine users typically binge on the drug until they are exhausted or run out of cocaine.

What Is Its Effect on the Mind?

The intensity of cocaine's euphoric effects depends on how quickly the drug reaches the brain, which depends on the dose and method of abuse. Following smoking or intravenous injection, cocaine reaches the brain in seconds, with a rapid buildup in levels. This results in a rapid-onset, intense euphoric effect known as a "rush."

By contrast, the euphoria caused by snorting cocaine is less intense and does not happen as quickly due to the slower build-up of the drug in the brain. Other effects include increased alertness and excitation, as well as restlessness, irritability, and anxiety.

Tolerance to cocaine's effects develops rapidly, causing users to take higher and higher doses. Taking high doses of cocaine or prolonged use, such as binging, usually causes paranoia. The crash that follows euphoria is characterized by mental and physical exhaustion, sleep, and depression lasting several days. Following the crash, users experience a craving to use cocaine again.

What Is Its Effect on the Body?

Physiological effects of cocaine include increased blood pressure and heart rate, dilated pupils, insomnia, and loss of appetite. The widespread abuse of highly pure street cocaine has led to many severe adverse health consequences such as:

- Cardiac arrhythmias,
- ischemic heart conditions,
- sudden cardiac arrest,
- convulsions,
- strokes,
- and death

In some users, the long-term use of inhaled cocaine has led to a unique respiratory syndrome, and chronic snorting of cocaine has led to the erosion of the upper nasal cavity.

Which Drugs Cause Similar Effects?

Other stimulants, such as methamphetamine, cause effects similar to cocaine that vary mainly in degree.

What Is Its Legal Status in the United States?

Cocaine is a Schedule II drug under the Controlled Substances Act, meaning it has a high potential for abuse and limited medical usage. Cocaine hydrochloride solution (4% and 10%) is used primarily as a topical local anesthetic for the upper respiratory tract. It also is used to reduce bleeding of the mucous membranes in the mouth, throat, and nasal cavities. However, better products have been developed for these purposes, and cocaine is rarely used medically in the United States.

METHAMPHETAMINE

What Is Methamphetamine?

Methamphetamine (meth) is a stimulant. The FDA-approved brand-name medication is Desoxyn®.

What Is Its Origin?

Mexican drug trafficking organizations have become the primary manufacturers and distributors of methamphetamine to cities throughout the United States, including in Hawaii. Domestic clandestine laboratory operators also produce and distribute meth but usually on a smaller scale. The methods used depend on the availability of precursor chemicals.

Currently, meth is mainly made with diverted products that contain pseudoephedrine. The Combat Methamphetamine Epidemic Act of 2005 requires retailers of non-prescription products containing pseudoephedrine, ephedrine, or phenylpropanolamine to place these products behind the counter or in a locked cabinet. Consumers must show identification and sign a logbook for each purchase.

What Are Common Street Names?

Common street names include:

- Batu,
- Bikers Coffee,
- Black Beauties,
- Chalk,
- Chicken Feed,
- Crank,
- Crystal,
- Glass,
- Go-Fast,
- Hiropon,
- ice,
- Meth,
- Methlies Quick,
- Poor Man's Cocaine,
- Shabu,
- Shards,
- Speed,
- Stove Top,
- Tina,
- Trash,
- Tweak,
- Uppers,
- Ventana,
- Vidrio,
- Yaba,
- and Yellow Bam

What Does It Look Like?

Regular meth is a pill or powder. Crystal meth resembles glass fragments or shiny blue-white "rocks" of various sizes.

How Is It Abused?

Meth is swallowed, snorted, injected, or smoked. To intensify the effects, users may take higher doses of the drug, take it more frequently, or change their method of intake.

In some cases, meth abusers go without food and sleep while taking part in a form of binging known as a "run." Meth users on a "run" inject as much as a gram of the drug every two to three hours over several days until they run out of meth or become too disorganized to continue.

What Is Its Effect on the Mind?

Meth is a highly addictive drug with potent central nervous system (CNS) stimulant properties.

Those who smoke or inject it report a brief, intense sensation, or rush. Oral ingestion or snorting produces a long-lasting high instead of a rush, which reportedly can continue for as long as half a day. Both the rush and the high are believed to result from the release of very high levels of the neurotransmitter dopamine into areas of the brain that regulate feelings of pleasure. Long-term meth use results in many damaging effects, including addiction.

Chronic meth abusers exhibit violent behavior, anxiety, confusion, insomnia, and psychotic features including paranoia, aggression, visual and auditory hallucinations, mood disturbances, and delusions — such as the sensation of insects creeping on or under the skin. Such paranoia can result in homicidal or suicidal thoughts. Researchers have reported that as much as 50% of the dopamine-producing cells in the brain can be damaged after prolonged exposure to relatively low levels of meth. Researchers also have found that serotonin-containing nerve cells may be damaged even more extensively.

What Is Its Effect on the Body?

Taking even small amounts of meth can result in:

- increased wakefulness,
- increased physical activity,
- decreased appetite,
- rapid breathing and heart rate,
- irregular heartbeat,
- increased blood pressure,
- and hyperthermia (overheating)

High doses can elevate body temperature to dangerous, sometimes lethal, levels, and cause convulsions and even cardiovascular collapse and death. Meth abuse may also cause extreme anorexia, memory loss, and severe dental problems.

What Are Its Overdose Effects?

High doses may result in death from stroke, heart attack, or multiple organ problems caused by overheating.

Which Drugs Cause Similar Effects?

Cocaine and potent stimulant pharmaceuticals, such as amphetamines and methylphenidate, produce similar effects.

What Is Its Legal Status in the United States?

Methamphetamine is a Schedule II stimulant under the Controlled Substances Act, which means that it has a high potential for abuse and limited medical use. It is available only through a prescription that cannot be refilled. Today there is only one legal meth product, Desoxyn®. It is currently marketed in 5-milligram tablets and has very limited use in the treatment of obesity and attention deficit hyperactivity disorder (ADHD).

MARIJUANA/CANNABIS

What Is Marijuana?

Marijuana is a mind-altering (psychoactive) drug, produced by the Cannabis sativa plant. Marijuana contains over 480 constituents. THC (delta-9-tetrahydrocannabinol) is believed to be the main ingredient that produces the psychoactive effect.

What Is Its Origin?

Marijuana is grown in the United States, Canada, Mexico, South America, and Asia. It can be cultivated in both outdoor and in indoor settings.

What Are Common Street Names?

Common street names include:

- Aunt Mary,
- BC Bud,
- Blunts,
- Boom,
- Chronic,
- Dope,
- Gangster,
- Ganja,
- Grass,
- Hash,
- Herb,
- Hydro,
- indo,
- Joint,
- Kif,
- Mary Jane,
- Mota,
- Pot,
- Reefer,
- Sinsemilla,
- Skunk,
- Smoke,
- Weed,
- and Yerba

What Does It Look Like?

Marijuana is a dry, shredded green/brown mix of flowers, stems, seeds, and leaves from the Cannabis sativa plant. The mixture typically is green, brown, or gray in color and may resemble tobacco.

How Is It Abused?

Marijuana is usually smoked as a cigarette (called a joint) or in a pipe or bong. It is also smoked in blunts, which are cigars that have been emptied of tobacco and refilled with marijuana, sometimes in combination with another drug. Marijuana is also mixed with foods or brewed as a tea.

What Is Its Effect on the Mind?

When marijuana is smoked, the THC passes from the lungs and into the bloodstream, which carries the chemical to the organs throughout the body, including the brain. In the brain, the THC connects to specific sites called cannabinoid receptors on nerve cells and influences the activity of those cells.

Many of these receptors are found in the parts of the brain that influence:

- Pleasure,
- memory,
- thought,
- concentration,
- sensory and time perception,
- and coordinated movement

The short-term effects of marijuana include:

- Problems with memory and learning, distorted perception, difficulty in thinking and problem-solving, and loss of coordination

The effect of marijuana on perception and coordination are responsible for serious impairments in learning, associative processes, and psychomotor behavior (driving abilities). Long term, regular use can lead to physical dependence and withdrawal following discontinuation, as well as psychic addiction or dependence.

Clinical studies show that the physiological, psychological, and behavioral effects of marijuana vary among individuals and present a list of common responses to cannabinoids, as described in the scientific literature:

- Dizziness, nausea, tachycardia, facial flushing, dry mouth and tremor initially
- Merriment, happiness, and even exhilaration at high doses
- Disinhibition, relaxation, increased sociability, and talkativeness
- Enhanced sensory perception, giving rise to increased appreciation of music, art, and touch
- Heightened imagination leading to a subjective sense of increased creativity
- Time distortions illusions, delusions, and hallucinations are rare except at high doses impaired judgment, reduced coordination, and ataxia, which can impede driving ability or lead to an increase in risk-taking behavior
- Emotional lability, incongruity of affect, dysphoria, disorganized thinking, inability to converse logically, agitation, paranoia, confusion, restlessness, anxiety, drowsiness, and panic attacks may occur, especially in inexperienced users or in those who have taken a large dose increased appetite and short-term memory impairment are common

Researchers have also found an association between marijuana use and an increased risk of depression, an increased risk and earlier onset of schizophrenia, and other psychotic disorders, especially for teens that have a genetic predisposition.

What Is Its Effect on the Body?

Short-term physical effects from marijuana use may include:

- Sedation,
- blood shot eyes,
- increased heart rate,
- coughing from lung irritation,
- increased appetite,
- and decreased blood pressure

Like tobacco smokers, marijuana smokers experience serious health problems such as bronchitis, emphysema, and bronchial asthma. Extended use may cause suppression of the immune system. Because marijuana contains toxins and carcinogens, marijuana smokers increase their risk of cancer of the head, neck, lungs, and respiratory tract.

Withdrawal from chronic use of high doses of marijuana causes physical signs including headache, shakiness, sweating, and stomach pains and nausea.

Withdrawal symptoms also include behavioral signs such as:

- Restlessness,
- irritability,
- sleep difficulties,
- and decreased appetite

Leaf of marijuana plant

What Are Its Overdose Effects?

No death from overdose of marijuana has been reported.

Which Drugs Cause Similar Effects?

Hashish and hashish oil are drugs made from the cannabis plant that are like marijuana, only stronger.

Hashish (hash) consists of the THC-rich resinous material of the cannabis plant, which is collected, dried, and then compressed into a variety of forms, such as balls, cakes, or cookie like sheets. Pieces are then broken off, placed in pipes or mixed with tobacco and placed in pipes or cigarettes, or smoked. The main sources of hashish are the Middle East, North Africa, Pakistan, and Afghanistan.

Hashish Oil (hash oil, liquid hash, cannabis oil) is produced by extracting the cannabinoids from the plant material with a solvent. The color and odor of the extract will vary, depending on the solvent used. A drop or two of this liquid on a cigarette is equal to a single marijuana joint. Like marijuana, hashish and hashish oil are both Schedule I drugs.

What Is Its Legal Status in the United States?

Marijuana is a Schedule I substance under the Controlled Substances Act, meaning that it has a high potential for abuse, no currently accepted medical use in treatment in the United States, and a lack of accepted safety for use under medical supervision.

Marinol, a synthetic version of THC, the active ingredient found in the marijuana plant, can be prescribed for the control of nausea and vomiting caused by chemotherapeutic agents used in the treatment of cancer and to stimulate appetite in AIDS patients. Marinol is a Schedule III substance under the Controlled Substances Act.

INDEX

C

D

E

F

G

H

I

J

L

M

N

O

P